July 9, 2009

To Melvin, may God

bless you always.

[signature]

Sacred Ground

Joyce Ann Whitlock

authorHOUSE®

AuthorHouse™
1663 Liberty Drive, Suite 200
Bloomington, IN 47403
www.authorhouse.com
Phone: 1-800-839-8640

First published by AuthorHouse 9/9/2008

ISBN: 978-1-4389-1594-4 (sc)
ISBN: 978-1-4389-1593-7 (hc)

Library of Congress Control Number: 2008908239

Printed in the United States of America
Bloomington, Indiana

This book is printed on acid-free paper.

Foreword

Sacred Ground is the true story of the lives of African-American families living in a small community during the early thirties through the twenty-first century. This book describes the resilience of these families in spite of the tragedies they experienced. Each family was unique, but one thing they all had in common was their deep-rooted faith in God. Cemeteries surround this small community; so many, that if the cemeteries were an ocean, the community could be considered a peninsula.

This community could easily be overlooked as a small group of plebeians who once lived there, but this would be the farthest from the truth. These individuals who lived here were wise, they were entrepreneurs, educators, parishioners, truck builders, investors, assisted in the assembling of the B-52 bomber during World War II. But most of all, they refused to die. It is their sprits that linger on this scared ground. For those of us who were fortunate having been reared in this community shall cherish this ground for generations.

Though this small community is located less than six miles from downtown Atlanta, the home of the former civil rights leader, Dr. Martin Luther King, Jr, these families were subjected the racial fury of the deep South in the 1950s. From having burning crosses thrown in their yards that continued from the early fifties until the early sixties by Klansmen to dealing with personal losses and the daily struggle of trying to make ends meet when average earning was $3.00 a day. But they were successful because they stood united and they prayed vehemently for one another.

This community is fading even as I write this book. Developers have begun to tear down homes that are symbols and fibers of our history, especially those of us who are indigenous to this community. I have tried to preserve some of our history by spearheading the renaming of two of the streets as a means of paying homage to those individuals who once lived there and who made great contributions to the community. It is this very community that shaped each of our lives to become productive citizens. It is this community that taught us values and embedded in our conscious those basic moral principles. Those who were reared in this sacred community are privileged to have such rich history of our ancestors, friends, and neighbors. I write this book with great honor and a sense of pride because I am a product of this community that sits on *Sacred Ground.*

Ðedication

• To Aunt Lucy, who stood by my side throughout the years

• A close friend, and confidante who gave me the concept to write this story.

• Mother and father who instilled those basic principles that shaped me to become the individual I am today; and who made it possible for me to reside in this sacred place.

• Myra Holmes who always took the time to read each chapter.

• Special friend, William Webb, who is always there to comment on any of my writings.

Acknowledgements

• My close friend, and confidante who gave me the concept to compose this novel.

• My brother, Hank, who inspired me to write this novel. My sisters, Ann, and Barbara and my brothers Herman and Robert who encouraged me by listening to me as I wrote each chapter.

• My mother and father who are now resting with the Lord. They instilled those basic principles that shaped me to becoming the individual I am today and who made it possible for me to reside in this sacred place to reflect on those earlier years where so much love was administered. May they rest in peace.

• Special acknowledgement to Myra Holmes who took the time to read

Table of Contents

Chapter 1

Prune Face: The Witch Doctor

I grew up in a suburban area of Atlanta, Georgia. I would say I had a happy childhood, surrounded by four older siblings and one younger sibling. My aunt and grandparents lived in the same neighborhood. But I would be remiss if I did not include one nosy neighbor, whom we called "Prune Face." She was just as much a part of the family as my biological brothers and sisters. We gave her this nickname because there was a cartoon character she resembled. She was short and had a broad face and a stocky build. She always wore a scarf around her head, and her daily attire consisted of an old, faintly colored dress made of flour sackcloth, and an old, faded floral apron. She wore high-top, laced shoes with thick, opaque stockings. We never knew Prune Face's age for two reasons. First, she would not tell you; and second, she would pluck out the gray as it grew around her hairline. My mother gave Prune Face complete authority to spank us, monitor our whereabouts, and get rid of any unauthorized guests who may have stumbled by during my mother's absence.

The back of Prune Face's house was very low to the ground compared to front of her house. Looking back, I believe that part of her house was an unfinished basement. The only thing that separated our house from Prune Face's house was a vacant lot, which made both houses sit approximately one hundred feet apart. Prune Face's kitchen was located on the backside, and her kitchen window faced our back door, which was our main entrance to our house. So, Prune Face had a direct view each time we entered or exited. One time while my mom was at work, she called Prune Face after she had been unsuccessful in reaching us by phone. She asked Prune Face if she had seen us. Prune Face explained that she had seen Beverly, Anita, and Harry (my siblings) walking to the basketball court. As the conversation was about to conclude, she remembered Harry was eating a sandwich.

Prune Face never worked from the time I can remember. She was a devoted housewife. Her husband, Robbin, was over six feet tall. He was a very heavily built man with a dark complexion. He had nine fingers and about ten yellow, dingy teeth. We never knew why the index finger of his left hand was missing, and he would never tell you, no matter how many times you asked. I remember one Christmas he came to our house in a Santa Claus costume. We knew it was Robbin because of his missing finger. His daily attire was coveralls, except for Sundays when he attended church. On Sundays, he would be seen wearing his navy blue suit and white shirt and navy blue tie. Robbin was very active in church; he served as an usher.

Robbin and Prune Face had one grown son together. Prune Face had one son from a previous marriage. After working all week, Robbin gave all of his week's earnings to Prune Face, who managed the household affairs. She, in return, gave him a weekly allowance. Of course, this arrangement was most challenging, as Robbin smoked and liked to drink moonshine to wind down after getting up all week at 5:00 in the morning. Prune Face disapproved of Robbin's drinking habit. Because of her disapproval, Robbin hid the liquor outside in a green patchy area near the outdoor toilet. Each time he excused himself to go to the toilet, he would take a detour and go to his secret place. He would look around to see if anyone was watching, then he would turn up the bottle and take a big swig. By the time he attempted to return to the house, he could hardly make it back. This went on for years. One day, Beverly and Anita (my older siblings) decided to teach him a lesson. One summer day, they waited until Robbin left for work. After he left, the two of them went to his secret place, poured out his moonshine, and replaced it with vinegar. Later that evening, when Robbin returned from work, he walked to his secret place. He turned up the bottle to take his usual big swig. But this time he spat out the content, because he realized it was not his liquor. He immediately began to focus his attention on our backyard. Perhaps he would have never known my sisters were the culprits, but they could not contain themselves from laughing until Robbin heard them. The following day, Robbin told mother what had happened. My two sisters received the worst spanking imaginable.

Years passed, and Robbin developed a chronic cough. In the fall of 1970, his coughing became so severe it caused him to choke after each episode. Prune Face would tell him, "You keep on coughing until you are going to go to the bathroom in your clothes." Robbin's cough worsened, and his son drove him to a local hospital. After a series of tests, he was diagnosed with lung cancer. I imagine the numerous years Robbin smoked those unfiltered cigarettes finally caught up with him. He underwent weeks of radiation therapy. Yet, his condition worsened until he became bedridden. This was taxing for Prune Face. All of a sudden, she had to take care of a man who had always been independent, as well as the breadwinner. Now the role was reversed.

On Thanksgiving morning in 1970, at approximately 10:00 a.m.,

Prune Face came to our house. She pleaded with my mother to return to her house because, "Something has happened to Robbin." Once my mother entered Robbin's bedroom, she realized he had died. Robbin's head was turned to the right, and his mouth was open. Mother consoled Prune Face and proceeded to call the local authorities. I felt so sad that Robbin died on Thanksgiving Day. I couldn't imagine the emptiness Prune Face must have felt having to suddenly live alone. Mother insisted I assist Prune Face with the funeral arrangements, such as making out the funeral program and any other matters for which she needed assistance. During the funeral, I had to read the obituary. Moreover, I had to read all of the cards attached to the flowers from individuals expressing their condolences. Back then, I feared attending funerals, not to mention standing beside Robbin's casket. That gave me the jitters!

Prune Face lived five years after the death of Robbin. She died of community-acquired pneumonia at the same hospital where Robbin had been treated. Late one summer day in 1975, neighbors became alarmed when they realized Prune Face, who usually worked daily in her yard, had not been seen for nearly a week. Two of them decided to pay her a visit. They found Prune Face in bed, covered with numerous homemade patch quilts. My mother was notified of Prune Face's sudden illness, and as usual, she asked me to go check on her. At that time, I had completed my nursing training, and my mother felt I would know just what to do for Prune Face. On entering Prune Face's dark bedroom, I saw two frail, elderly, African-American women surrounding Prune Face. She had fallen while attempting to go to the bathroom. When I tried to put her back in bed, one of the elderly neighbors became hostile, insisting that she could put Prune Face back in bed independently. But she soon realized Prune Face was much too heavy for her to handle. I finally convinced her that I had the skills and the strength to get Prune back in bed.

Once Prune Face was back in bed, I noticed she was trembling. She wanted additional blankets on a hot August day, with a temperature soaring close to 90 degrees. I took her temperature the best I could, since Prune Face couldn't keep her mouth closed because of the shivering. Even under those conditions, Prune Face's temperature measured 103 degrees Fahrenheit. I knew immediately she had to be transported to the hospital, so I called the local county emergency response unit. Twenty minutes later, two county firefighters came in with their emergency kit. One of them was a very tall, thin man, who looked as though he was in his early thirties. The second firefighter appeared to be no more than eighteen years old. He was the more vocal of the two. He asked many questions, but Prune Face couldn't answer any of them because of her shivering.. He turned to the two elderly women and asked them to describe exactly what happened to Prune Face. Surprisingly, the two elderly women were mesmerized. The one who had been so hostile toward me and had been so vociferous suddenly could not speak. Perhaps these two elderly African-American women witnessed Klu Klux Klansmen throwing crosses in their yards, and maybe they were just too afraid to speak, or maybe they had been taught all of their lives to remain silent in the presence of a Caucasian, especially those who wore uniforms. So, I began to answer the questions, explaining what had transpired to the best of my knowledge. Afterward, the firefighter explained to us that Prune Face's condition was not an emergency, and there was nothing they could do. He never examined Prune Face, and yet he made the decision her condition was not an emergency. That is when I reached my boiling point. I asked him whether an individual with a temperature of 103 degrees was sick enough to transport to the hospital. The teenage-looking firefighter proceeded to take Prune Face's temperature. By then, Prune Face temperature had risen to 103.8 degrees. Suddenly, the room became silent. The firefighters looked at each other, walked into the other room, and begin to whisper to each other. After concluding their conversation, they returned to the bedroom. The teenage-looking firefighter asked me what local hospital I preferred.

I remembered Prune Face and her son had taken Robbin to the

public hospital in Atlanta. Moreover, I was employed at that same hospital. By now, I had calmed down considerably, especially since I knew the firefighter recognized Prune Face's condition was serious. I politely suggested that they transport her to the public city hospital in Atlanta.

After the firefighters transported Prune Face, I took charge. I directed one of the two elderly neighbors to notify Prune Face's son of her condition, and I assured them both that I would visit Prune Face once I returned to work. The neighbor who had been hostile remained silent as she walked away somberly.

The following day, my sister Anita and I decided to visit Prune Face at the hospital. We knew Prune Face had never spent one night away from home, and she had never been admitted to a hospital. Midwives delivered all of her children at home. Once we arrived at the hospital, we observed a nurse sitting at the nurse's station. We asked for Prune Face's room number, and she directed us to a four-bed ward. The ward was very hot, because there was no air conditioning in the hospital. Prune Face was in the third bed; the curtain was drawn, separating her from the patient in the next bed. The room had a very foul odor. Once Prune Face saw my sister and me, she exclaimed, "Here are my girls." She proceeded to explain to the other patients in the room how she had raised us. Looking back, I realize Prune Face was merely validating that she had earned the right to claim us as her own children. While I sat at her bedside, I reflected on those earlier years when Prune Face ran unauthorized guests from our house during my mother's absence, and the times she barged into our house unannounced while we were watching our favorite cartoons and demanded we change the channel so she could watch her soap operas. I also recalled that when we had minor burns, we would run to Prune Face's house for her to talk the fire out of the affected area. Analyzing Prune Face's actions today, I realize Prune Face may have been involved in witchcraft. She would bend down to the burned area, and for approximately five minutes, she would chant. Prune Face never told anyone what she said during this ritual. One thing for sure, we felt better afterward. Perhaps this was all psychological. I reflected on those times Prune Face had created a makeshift store in her home when she and Robbin experienced hard times. She sold candy and soft drinks to the children in the community. I remember how she would scold us whenever we brought her pennies. Now, as I think back, perhaps the reason Prune Face disliked pennies was because her vision was impaired, and it was difficult for her to differentiate pennies from the other coins. I thought how Prune Face had kept my younger sibling and me when we were underage for primary school. I remember she would serve us freshly cooked collard greens from her garden for lunch. For dessert, she would give us graham crackers and bananas. Now, there lay Prune Face in the hospital, helpless and dependent on others to assist her with her basic needs.

The day after my sister and I visited Prune Face, my mother received a phone call from one of the neighbors informing her that Prune Face had died. I thought how could that happened within twenty-four hours; she was so vibrant during our visit.

Prune Face had a very simple funeral. Again, my mother asked me to assist the family in planning the funeral service. Prune Face had two sisters who were up in age and frail. They came to Prune Face's house and went through everything she and Robbin had accumulated over their lifetime. They snatched goods so fast, they took my vacuum cleaner I had offered them to assist in cleaning the house for expected guests. I had to call one of the sisters to tell her she had inadvertently taken my vacuum. She had to drive some twenty miles to return it. It was so sad to think that Prune Face's family's chief concern was to obtain her earthly possessions.

The community was never the same after the deaths of Prune Face and Robbin. The house was rented to various individuals and eventually torn down. Today, just a vacant lot remains. The things left to remind us that Prune Face and Robbin existed includes the same leaning, silver, rusty mailbox Robbin would lean on as he retrieved the mail each evening before retiring. Still standing tall is an oak tree that once provided shade for Prune Face and Robbin as they sat on the front porch during the hot summer months. This is sacred ground.

Chapter 2

Mr. & Mrs Walsh: The Odd Couple

The neighbors who lived next door to our left were a childless couple. They were Mr. and Mrs. Walsh. They were most odd. They could be defined as a reclusive couple. Their house sat on one and one and one-fourth acres of land enclosed by a six-foot chain-link fence. To ensure they maintained their privacy, and to prevent any intruders, they installed burglar bars on every window. In addition, the window screens were painted with silver paint to prevent anyone from seeing inside.

Mrs. Walsh was a very tall woman, approximately 6′ tall, and Mr. Walsh was relatively short compared to Mrs. Walsh; he was about 5′7″. Mrs. Walsh, regardless of the season of the year, would wear long, cotton dresses with an apron, and she wore a bonnet. She looked as if she was part Cherokee Indian. She had very high cheekbones, and her eyes were very small and slanted. Yet, because of her attire, she looked very much like an Amish woman of the Pennsylvania countryside. Mr. Walsh wore coveralls and a wide-brim hat. He was a very docile man. By today's standards, he would be viewed as a henpecked husband, because Mrs. Walsh was in charge. When there was yard work to be done, Mrs. Walsh—hands on her hips—stood over her husband as if she were his supervisor, to ensure the task was done to her specifications. Mrs. Walsh never learned to drive, so Mr. Walsh drove her everywhere she needed to go. They had an orchard of plum, apple, and peach trees on their one and one-fourth acre of land. During the summer months, you could smell the fresh ripe peaches and plums throughout the community. The children in the community were always at their fence, pleading for Mrs. Walsh to come out to give them a bag of fruit. Mrs. Walsh would ignore them and seldom came out of their house regardless of how loud the children became. But if Mrs. Walsh wanted information about the latest community gossip, she would come to greet them and give them as much fruit as they could carry. Of course, this was after they had engaged in a lengthy conversation. My mother and father ordered us not to ask for any of Mr. and Mrs. Walsh's fruit. We were even forbidden to look at the Walsh house in any way that might suggest we desired their fruit. And bedsides, we had our own orchard of fruits such as apple, peach, fig, and cherry trees. Since the Walshes refused to be generous in giving the children fruit, the children would wait until nightfall, then climb over the fence and get as much fruit as their heart desired. You could hear limbs breaking as they removed the fruit. Sometimes the Walshes would watch for them and turn on their floodlights, but to no avail; the children were quicker than lightning. They would crawl to the back of the property and jump over the fence before the Walshes could catch them. Mr. and Mrs. Walsh would be furious. Mrs. Walsh would call the police. The police would take a report, but that was the extent of the officer's investigation. I imagine the police officer wondered why on earth the Walshes didn't just give the children the fruit. It was more than the Walshes could eat, and the fruit would eventually rot on the trees. This would go on for years. The Walshes were extremely nosy. My father worked out of town, leaving my mother with the awesome task of managing the household. I recalled one month during my father's absence, the Walshes wanted to keep up on our whereabouts. My mother was young and very attractive. The other neighbors were inquisitive, of course, but the Walshes were the most inquisitive. Each time we came home at night, the Walshes would turn their floodlights on our house. The lights were installed so they aimed directly on our house. Their lights were so bright, we didn't have to turn on the lights inside our house. One day, my mother decided to give the Walshes a taste of their own medicine. She had my uncle help her buy building materials, and she installed floodlights attached to tall poles aimed directly at the Walshes' house. At nightfall, my mother would say, "I think it's about time to let Mr. Walsh look at Mrs. Walsh," and she would turn on the lights. I imagine this was most disturbing, since the Walshes went to bed very early.

Early one morning, two weeks after my mother installed the lights, Mr. Walsh came to the fence and called for my mother. He told her, "Mrs. Whitlock, I laid my burden down. I am taking my lights down, and I won't turn them on your house anymore." He never asked my mother to remove our lights, but my mom explained to him that over the years, she had become annoyed at having their lights shine into our house. My mother decided to remove our lights as well.

Years passed, and Mr. Walsh was seldom seen (occasionally you would see him in the yard). It seemed so strange. One of the neighbors saw Mrs. Walsh and asked her how he was doing. She informed the neighbor that Mr. Walsh had died months earlier. How strange, because no one saw an undertaker or an ambulance. It was rumored that Mrs. Walsh had kept him tied in a chair after his death. One day while Mr. Walsh's son from a previous marriage decided to pay a visit, found his father's decomposed body.

After the death of Mr. Walsh, Mrs. Walsh became very lonely. She began to walk around the neighborhood, asking various neighbors to drive her to town. She began leaving the gate open, allowing the children to enter the compound at will to retrieve as much fruit as their hearts desired. Yet, sometimes Mrs. Walsh would remember to secure the gate, and she reverted to her stern demeanor. She began to call the police more frequently than ever. She became paranoid and disoriented. She began flagging down police officers to engage in a conversation whenever she saw them patrolling the neighborhood. Obviously, she was lonely.

In May 1989, a police officer driving through the community noticed Mrs. Walsh's gate was open. He proceeded down the long driveway, and he saw that her back door was also open. He entered the kitchen, then the bedroom. That is where he discovered Mrs. Walsh had been brutally murdered. There was blood all over her. An autopsy revealed she had been stabbed multiple times. The community was outraged, because this was a community where everyone knew each other and left their doors unlocked at night. A community meeting was held at the church, and a $1,000 reward was posted for anyone who would identify Mrs. Walsh's killer. Sadly, the killer remains at large. Many rumors were started, such as the murderer was an individual who once lived in the community but relocated to the north. There was nothing to substantiate that rumor.

I think back over the years when Mr. and Mrs. Walsh isolated themselves. No one would even think about visiting them. Yet, it was during those latter years, when Mrs. Walsh began to trust others, that she met her fate. The Walshes' house remains surrounded by the same chain-link fence. The fruit trees were destroyed by lightning strikes over the years. However, an oak tree, a pecan tree, and four tall Georgia pine trees remain. The community church owns the house. Ironically, for years, the public was forbidden from entering the Walshes' premises, and now the house serves as a transitional house for low-income families. The house has had some small improvements made, but the structure remains the same as it was when Mr. and Mrs. Walsh lived in it. After all, this is scared ground.

Chapter 3

Miss Whitsett: The Dance Hall

Miss Whitsett and her aging mother lived further down the street. Miss Whitsett was very dedicated in caring for her mother, who some said was well over a hundred years old. The mother was a frail woman who looked Caucasian. Miss Whitsett would braid her mother's snow-white hair, which reached down to her legs. As children, we would sit and watch her braid her mother's hair, because we were amazed to see such long hair. Miss Whitsett was a very tall woman, about six feet tall, and she weighed at least 180 pounds. She had hazel eyes, and like her mother, she had long hair; hers extended to her waist. She had a reddish complexion. As I think of her today, she, too, could have been Cherokee.

Years passed, and Miss Whitsett's mother died, leaving Miss Whitsett alone. But this would be only a brief period. Miss Whitsett met a man approximately six months after the death of her mother. This man undoubtedly needed a place to live. They married in a courthouse, but the marriage wouldn't last; it was rumored the man was gay. A divorce was pursued after they had been married for about a year. Miss Whitsett was a civic-minded woman. She was member of the local NAACP, and she urged neighbors to vote during local and national elections. If they didn't have transportation, she would pick them up and take them to the voting polls. Miss Whitsett was also an entrepreneur. She had a store with a jukebox, where teenagers in the community would go dance until nightfall (often exceeding my older siblings' curfew). Miss Whitsett loved children, and children felt the same way about her. She never looked down on the children, no matter how mischievous they were. Miss Whitsett was also prudent. She saved her money religiously and taught us to do the same. As time passed, Miss Whitsett became less mobile because of chronic arthritis that left her in a wheelchair. Even in a wheelchair, this woman was quite determined not to let anything defeat her. She continued to do her housework from the wheelchair. One day when I visited her, I was amazed to see her beautiful, shining, wooden floors, the starch tablecloth on her tables, and the sparkling figurines on the mantel. You would have thought she had a maid. Over the years, Mrs. Whitsett became so incapacitated her niece had no choice but to place her in a nursing home facility. During a conversation with my sister Anita one Sunday, I begin to reminisce about the many acts of kindness Miss Whitsett had done for the community, especially the way she treated the children with the makeshift dance hall for teenagers to dance until nightfall. So, we decided to visit her at the nursing facility. On arriving at the facility, we stopped at the nurse's station, introduced ourselves, and asked if we could visit with Miss Whitsett. The nurse responded, "Of course." She told us the room number and pointed in the direction of her room. As we walked down the hall, we observed numerous frail residents sitting in wheelchairs in the hall. Others were in their beds, and others were shouting out incoherently; some residents were gathered in a dayroom, listening to a sermon by a clergyman. When we entered Miss Whitsett's room, she was all alone, lying in bed and looking out of the window. When she saw us, her eyes illuminated, and she gave us the biggest smile. She uttered, "Well, I'll be. You Whitlock girls came to see me." I thought how awful it was for Ms. Whitsett, who was once independent and an entrepreneur, to find herself in a bedlam. I asked her if she would like to sit in a wheelchair so we could go sit outside, since it was such a beautiful spring day. She was initially reluctant, but after my sister convinced her how beneficial it would be, she agreed. It was taxing getting her into the wheelchair, because she had been confined to bed so long she could hardly stand. But we got her into the wheelchair and transported her to the garden outside. The garden was beautifully designed, with numerous assorted perennials and plenty of shady areas thanks to the tall oak trees. A statue of an angel stood in the middle of the garden. Our conversation was mostly small talk, but Miss Whitsett often redirected it to her desire to return to her home. Miss Whitsett told us her niece had taken complete control of her finances and had withdrawn most of her money from the bank. She told us she had put a stop to it by calling the bank from the nursing facility and forbidding her niece from making future withdrawals. She went on to tell us how she was placed in the nursing facility unwillingly. As Miss Whitsett spoke, I glanced at my sister and saw she had begun to cry. No matter how we tried to steer the conversation to another topic, Miss Whitsett continued to express her desire to return to her home. I didn't think it would hurt for her to at least see her home again. So I asked the charge nurse if she could contact her niece to obtain permission to take Miss Whitsett out for a short outing. The nurse called the niece and gave our names to the niece and asked her if we could take Miss Whitsett out for a ride. The niece consented, since we were well known in the community. Once we got Miss Whitsett in the car, we headed to her former community. As we rode, there was complete silence. Miss Whitsett just looked out of the window. Once we turned into Miss Whitsett's driveway, she began to perk up with excitement, as if to say, "I'm home at last." We thought just having Miss Whitsett look at her house from the car would be the extent of our outing, but Miss Whitsett insisted we go inside. My sister and I were surprised when Miss Whitsett opened her purse and, after searching and searching, pulled out a large, round, flat key. She instructed my sister to open the door and for me to assist her with her walker. After assisting her out of the car and to stand, I realized I had a challenge on my hands because she had been bedridden for months, Miss Whitsett was very weak. We eventually got her inside her house and assisted her to the living room. The dark mahogany wooden floors were in good condition, just as Miss Whitsett had left them. They were a bit dusty, but otherwise they were fine. Her furniture was still arranged as she had left it prior to entering the nursing facility. The coffee table in front of a sofa covered with an embroidered cloth was neatly arranged. In front of the fireplace was a figurine of a ceramic cat. Miss Whitsett loved cats, and I wondered what had happened to her cats. Perhaps the cats decided to leave to fend for themselves after months of neglect. We proceeded to the dining room, where four ladder-back chairs neatly surrounded an oversized dining-room table with a floral centerpiece. Miss Whitsett then instructed us to take her to the bedroom. The bedroom was very small. One full-size bed neatly made with a white bedspread. To the left was a small closet with an adjoining bathroom, where towels were neatly hanging. After a few seconds, Miss Whitsett said, "Let's go to the kitchen." As we went back through the dining room and proceeded to the kitchen, Miss Whitsett began to perspire profusely. Sweat appeared on her forehead and ran down to her neck. She became very weak, and I directed my sister to get a chair. We managed to place her down in the chair. I was relieved after Miss Whitsett was settled, because she was about to faint. After Miss Whitsett sat for a few minutes, I asked her if she was ready to return to the nursing facility. She said that she could stay alone. My sister explained that if she stayed, the local authorities would come after us. Anita also promised Miss Whitsett that, if she returned to the nursing facility, she would return in three days to check on her. Miss Whitsett finally agreed to return. The next challenge was getting her back to the car. But after small steps and frequent rest periods, we succeeded. Driving back, I thought, *If* I get Miss Whitsett back to the *nursing facility, I will never sign her out again.* As we drove back, there was complete silence. My sister and I were mentally and physically exhausted, so we couldn't engage in any conversation even if we wanted to. Miss Whitsett was fatigued. This was, after all, probably the most active she'd been in a very long time. Once we entered the compound of the nursing facility, Miss Whitsett appeared sad and gloomy. We retrieved a wheelchair, placed her in it, and transported her back to her room. We said our goodbyes and gave Miss Whitsett our phone numbers in the event she needed something. In the back of our minds, however, we were hoping she didn't call us anytime soon. On returning to the car, I reprimanded my sister, "Why did you promise her you would be returning in three days?" My sister laughed and said, "Well, I just told her that—anything to get her back to the nursing home." My sister and I realized we had made a mistake in taking Miss Whitsett back to her home. After all, we promised Miss Whitsett's niece we were just going sightseeing. The next week, my sister received a phone call from Miss Whitsett. Surprisingly, she was calling from her residence. She had put up such a fuss with the nursing facility's staff that they released her. She called to tell my sister she didn't have to visit her at the nursing facility because she had returned to her home. Anita and I felt we were to blame, that taking her back to her home might have caused Miss Whitsett to demand she be discharged from the nursing facility. One Sunday evening, two months after Miss Whitsett retuned to her home, my sister and I were talking at my kitchen's table when we heard the sirens of an emergency response vehicle followed by a fire truck. They proceeded to Miss Whitsett's street and parked in front of her driveway. My sister and I agreed that we should go see about Miss Whitsett. Once we arrived, we could hardly enter Miss Whitsett's small house because of the fire-fighters and emergency response team present in the small bedroom. Miss Whitsett was lying in bed, and her niece was at her bedside. One of the emergency response staff was administering oxygen and attempting to initiate intravenous fluids. Anita shouted, "Miss Whitsett, we are here, the Whitlock girls." Miss Whitsett looked up at us and said weakly, "Oh, hi." Her niece looked at us in dismay.

We asked her what had happened to Miss Whitsett. She explained she had tried to call her for two days, but Miss Whitsett failed to answer the phone. So she decided to come pay her a visit and discovered her aunt had been in bed for a week. The emergency response staff interrupted our conversation. He informed the niece that Miss Whitsett had to be transported to the hospital. Miss Whitsett had apparently suffered a heart attack. My sister and I left thinking that was the last time we would ever see Miss Whitsett. Yet, we were happy Miss Whitsett had an opportunity to leave the nursing facility and return to her home. Miss Whitsett remained in the hospital for two months. This was the same hospital where Prune Face died. Miss Whitsett died of complications due to pneumonia. My sister and I did not attend the funeral, because Miss Whitsett arranged for her body to be cremated. She told her neighbors the expense of having a funeral was incomprehensible, and the money could be put into a savings account. Miss Whitsett's estate was left to her niece. Anita and I speculated that Miss Whitsett had millions, since she was an entrepreneur and the most frugal person we had ever known. Miss Whitsett's small, single-family home remains just as if Miss Whitsett were alive. The small, stucco building where she sold drinks and candy was sold and later rented, but is now vacant on the property, just as Miss Whitsett left it. This is sacred ground.

Chapter 4

Mr. & Mrs. Allenson: The Relocators

Mr. and Mrs. Allenson lived next door to Miss Whitsett. They had three children. They were a hard-working couple, and they lived a private life. Their children attended the same public school as the children in the community, so the Allensons did have that one thing in common with the community. Yet, unlike the community, they did not attend the community Baptist church, which was located practically in front of their door. This was in the early fifties, and in the South, if an individual was not a Baptist affiliate, it was unusual—at least it was for the people in this small, rustic community. Mrs. Allenson's sister and brother-in-law lived next door, and Mrs. Allenson's mother, Mrs. Brinkley, lived across the street in a back house of the general store she operated daily. Mr. and Mrs. Allenson, and her sister and brother-in-law, would eventually move out of the community. Their houses remain just as they left them, some fifty years ago. There have been some minor improvements, but the houses' basic structures have not changed.

Mrs. Brinkley, Mrs. Allenson's mother, lived in the community until she died of old age. She was an obese woman with long, thick, black hair and a fair complexion. She kept her hair in braids, and even braided, it extended to her lower back. She really looked like an old Eskimo woman. She spoke with in very high-pitched voice. Mrs. Brinkley was integral to the community, because she operated a store where she sold penny wheel cookies, Tootsie Rolls, fried pork skins in a brown greasy bag, and cold sodas such as miniature bottles of Coke and Nehi.

Each day after school, the children in the community would run to Mrs. Brinkley's store. Mrs. Brinkley loved cats, so about five cats would constantly be found creeping around inside her store; they could be seen walking on the countertop. Mrs. Brinkley would pick them up and gently put them down on the floor and then wait on us, never stopping to wash her hands. Sometimes Mrs. Brinkley would be in a cranky mood. For instance, if you didn't have enough money to purchase an item, she would become furious. She would sit all day on the porch of the store, rocking back and forth in her rocking chair. When the children came to make purchases, she would lean forward several times in her attempt to get up from the chair. After a few seconds, she would finally rise and enter the store. If we asked for cookies, she would occassionally wash her hands in a round wash pan filled with filthy water that appeared to have been sitting all week. She then dried her hands on the old, dirty apron she wore. Then she would open a large plastic container full of cookies and reach in and retrieve the cookie(s).

Mrs. Brinkley died at a very old age. The store and her home were torn down. The property was sold, and a new home was built on this parcel. This is sacred ground.

Chapter 5

Mr. & Mrs. Smith: The Protectors

Mr. and Mrs. Smith had six children. They lived directly in front of the community church. This family was similar to my family, meaning that both families had three girls and three boys. Mr. Smith was a very short, obese man who could be seen on a hot summer day sitting topless on his porch. He worked as a mechanic at a local automobile plant. Mrs. Smith was very tall woman; in fact, she was taller than Mr. Smith. She was a domestic worker. One particular night, cars were heard riding through our community. They were the Klansmen, who decided—as they occasionally did—to drive through our community shouting racial remarks. At other times, they did more than drive by shouting racial remarks; they would throw burning crosses onto the yards of our small community. Mr. Smith, like so many other neighbors, was very brave and determined to protect his family. One night the Klansmen decided to come through our community speeding by on the dirt road, kicking up rocks, and shouting the "N" word. But this particular night, Mr. Smith had had enough. He gave his wife a loaded gun and ordered her to position herself in the bedroom. He armed himself with a shotgun and sat waiting in the front room of his house. He instructed her to shoot to kill if he were killed or if the intruders made it back into the bedroom. The Klansmen; were satisfied for having scarred the wits out of the neighbors in this small community. Perhaps the cemeteries that surrounded the neighborhood were a deterrent for what could have become a quagmire.

The Klansmen rode around the community throwing crosses in each family's yard at least every other month. Perhaps this was their initiation ceremony. They targeted the minister's house, especially since his house was the first one on the left as you entered the small community. Moreover, his mailbox listed his title, "Reverend," so you didn't have to be a rocket scientist to know he was the minister. But he was not alone. Mr. Jenkins, who was the head deacon at that time, would park in front of the minister's house all night, waiting for any aberrant behavior by the Klansmen. He, like my father, always stood ready to protect the community if the situation warranted. Years passed, and Mr. Smith died. Mrs. Smith lived some twenty years after the death of her husband, but as she aged, she became ill. All of her children were married and had moved out of the community. Yet, her second daughter became the matriarch of this family. She and husband moved in with Mrs. Smith and took care of her until she died. After the death of Mrs. Smith, the eldest sister became very ill, and she also moved back into the community, in a house across the street from the Smiths' homestead. The eldest sister's condition worsened, and she became bedridden. The middle sister was her primary caretaker until she died as a result of cerebrovascular disease. Twelve years after the eldest sister's death, the youngest sister succumbed in her sleep. The only surviving sister grieved but really could not get over the loss of her two sisters. In less than two years the youngest brother died. The surviving sister kept her faith in a much higher source. Last than a year, after losing her youngest brother, her eldest brother died suddenly. Now her only surviving sibling is one brother, who has liver disease. She now oversees his medical needs by ensuring he keeps his doctors' appointments and by transporting him to the nearest hospital's emergency room when his condition warrants. Moreover, she is called on to help in the church, such as singing a solo at church funerals and to cook and plan the church menu for the annual church homecoming. Also, she is asked to notify each neighbor in the neighborhood to attend monthly community meetings, and if the neighbors are unable to walk, she coordinates transportation, and sometimes she picks them up in her vehicle. She is truly an amazing woman.

Chapter 6

Mr. & Mrs. Budlong: Mr. Plumber

Mr. and Mrs. Budlong lived next door to the Smiths. The Budlongs was a childless couple. Mrs. Budlong worked as a maid at a local high school, and Mr. Budlong worked as a construction worker, where he acquired many skills in the home improvement business. Because of his skills, the people in the community would call him whenever they had a plumbing problem. He would charge them very little; sometimes he wouldn't charge a dime! Mrs. Budlong had a sister who became quite ill. Mrs. Budlong moved her sister into her home and became her sister's primary caretaker. Years earlier, Mrs. Budlong was the primary caretaker for her mother, who died in her care. Caring for her sister was quite taxing, because she would have alcohol withdrawal seizures as a result of her alcoholism. After a long illness, Mrs. Budlong's sister died. Thirty years later, Mrs. Budlong had a stroke was hospitalized in a nearby hospital. Mr. Budlong was preparing to visit Mrs. Budlong at the hospital when he began to have chest pains. Mrs. Budlong's relatives, who were visiting, called the ambulance. On Mr. Budlong's arrival at the emergency room, he was pronounced dead. Mrs. Budlong, still recuperating from her stroke, had to be informed her husband had had a sudden heart attack and died. How tragic. Mrs. Budlong attended her husband's funeral confined to a wheelchair. Mrs. Budlong lived fifteen years after the death of her husband. After her his death, she lived life to the fullest. She enjoyed eating at various restaurants daily and attending church on Sundays. I attended a funeral of one of the neighbors, and Mrs. Budlong was in attendance. Immediately afterward, she said, "Let's go out to eat." I was very low on funds, and I told her let me take a rain check. I promised to take her and another church member out the following Sunday. She quickly responded, "Oh, just you and me," because she never has any "chain chain." The following Sunday, I was too tired to go anywhere after working so hard the week prior. So, I sent a message to one of the church members to inform Mrs. Budlong that I would call her to reschedule. The next week I sold my car, which had proven to be a lemon. I promised the Lord if he allowed me to obtain my dream car, Mrs. Budlong and the other church member would be the first to ride in my new car. Sure enough, that week I drove off with my new car. The following Sunday, I drove up to the door of the church so it would be easy for Mrs. Budlong and the other church member to get into my car. (Mrs. Budlong was dependent on a walker after her stroke, which left her weak. In addition, she had Parkinson's disease. The other church member was morbidly obese, making it more difficult for her to get into my car than it was for Mrs. Budlong.)

One fall day in 2007 Mrs. Budlong experienced breathing difficulties. The emergency response team was called, but they never came. A relative decided to drive Mrs. Budlong to the hospital, but Mrs. Budlong died en route. I didn't attend Mrs. Budlong's funeral, because I wanted to remember her the last time we went out to eat. Mrs. Budlong's beautiful ranch home was left to her niece. It is just as though Mrs. Budlong were still alive. This is sacred ground.

Chapter 7

Mr. & Mrs. Beechers: The Beecher Family

Next door to Mr. and Mrs. Budlong were Mr. and Mrs. Beechers. They had two sons. The older of the two was nearly seven feet tall, and the youngest son stood about six feet tall. He was autistic. Both their sons worked as janitors at a local hospital. They were different as day and night. For example, the youngest son worked until he reached the age of retirement. But the oldest son went into the military, and after his return, he became an alcoholic. Eventually he succumbed to liver disease. After the death of Mr. Beechers, Mrs. Beechers relied on the elder son to assist her with financial matters. Little did she know, this son withdrew most of her money to support his drinking.

Mrs. Beechers eventually became so ill from diabetes that she had to be placed in a nursing facility. She died a year later. The youngest son lives alone. He depends on distant cousins to administer his monthly check and to oversee his financial affairs. One day he was so upset he came to my house. He said his cousin told him he was going to be placed in nursing home. I smelled alcohol on his breath, and I guess that was what gave him the nerve to come to me to complain. In the past, he would volunteer to help me clean the community, and he assisted by bringing chairs when there were community meetings. Perhaps he felt I was the only person whom he could rely on. Of course, I sent him back to discuss the matter with his cousins. As he was leaving, I began to reminisce how, on New Year's Day, this individual would walk in every room of everyone's house in the neighborhood. This is a southern tradition. It is believed to be good luck if a man first enters an individual's home on New Year's Day, and especially if he walks in every room of the house. How sad to see this man now living alone.

Chapter 8

Mr. & Mrs. Ansley: The Love Birds

Next door to the Beechers was a couple with five children. Mr. and Mrs. Ansley. Mrs. Ansley had been married prior and had three adult children from the first marriage. This couple was the most humorous one in the neighborhood (Robbin and Prune Face were his parents) because some days they were seen holding hands kissing in public and the next day or so they were fighting.

Ms. Ansley worked as a cook at a local, well-known restaurant. Mr. Ansley worked as a ditch digger for a local plumbing company. At the end of the week, they wanted to celebrate and relax after their long arduous week. But, it would result in the two of them getting into a brawl, her stabbing him, and having to call 911. This went on for years. Ms. Ansley knew I was a nurse, so she would call me to remove Mr. Ansley's sutures after they had been in place for a week. One time after I had removed the sutures, she asked me, "What do I owe you?" I responded, "Nothing. Just don't cut him again." Summer 1981, Ms. Ansley received a phone call early one morning. She was informed her youngest daughter had been stabbed to death in a nearby town. Ms. Ansley was never the same after the death of her daughter. She began to drink excessively, and she died as a result of alcohol abuse. She left behind her husband and a seven-year-old son.

After Mrs. Ansley's death, Mr. Ansley began to drink excessively. He would sometimes drink until he was so inebriated he could not make it home. He would sleep at the side of the road in the community. How sad. The son grew up without a mother, and his father was unable to provide for him. As a result, the son was in and out of jail, became a teenage father, and eventually dropped out of high school. A grown son from Mrs. Ansley's previous marriage would come by occasionally to look in on his half brother and stepfather. But he couldn't help them, because he had a drug addiction that would eventually kill him. After this son's death, Mr. Ansley became ill. His brother consulted with me about his brother's condition. No one had seen Mr. Ansley for weeks. The brother forced himself inside the house and discovered Mr. Ansley was bedridden and had not eaten for days. Being the nurse in the community, I recommended he call the ambulance to transport him to the local hospital (the same hospital his father and mother— Prune Face and Robbin—were treated). He underwent a battery of tests in the hospital. The physician diagnosed him with throat cancer and gave him six months to live. Mr. Ansley died at a hospice within three months of his diagnosis. Today, the Ansley house is boarded up, and viewing this house brings back memories of the many tragedies this family encountered. This is sacred ground.

Chapter 9

Mr. & Mrs. James: The Disciplinarian

Mr. and Mrs. James lived next door to the Ansleys. These two families were related: Mrs. James was Mrs. Ansley's mother. Mrs. James was about four feet tall, and she weighed approximately two hundred pounds. She waddled when she walked. She always wore a scarf around her head, a sackcloth dress, and an old faded apron. Mrs. James was a stay-at-home mom. Mr. James worked in a nearby mill. He was a very tall man who wore coveralls every day. Mrs. James was quite religious. She demanded everyone in the household attend church on Sunday. My grandmother lived directly across the street from the James family. I didn't attend kindergarten (my parents couldn't afford it), so my aunt, who lived with my grandmother, babysat my brother and me. We had to play outside most of the day, unless it was a rainy day. All day I could hear Mrs. James banging on the piano (she never took piano lessons) and singing gospel songs. I think my aunt was so tired of hearing Ms. James playing the piano so she turned the volume up on her radio. One can imagine that the environment became a bedlam for those who were nearby. Looking back, I imagine Mrs. James was using the piano to drown out the frustration and the deep internal pain she must have felt. Mrs. James was nice to my brother and me; she would invite us into her house.

As the years went by, Mr. James died, leaving Mrs. James with five children and a cow. I remember she was a strict disciplinarian, more so after the death of her husband. She would call her children's names out in a loud voice when she wanted them to do a specific chore. Her nephew lived with them for a short while. He was responsible for taking the cow out to graze during the day and before nightfall; he was to bring the cow back home. Sometimes that cow would break away, and Mrs. James would call the nephew's name so loudly everyone in the community could hear her. She would shout, "Billie, Billie, you better go and get that cow." As the years passed, Mrs. James developed a heart condition, and she later developed breast cancer. She received monthly examinations at the cardiac clinic, which was located in the hospital where I was employed as a nurse. She was so proud of me, especially because we lived in the same community. She would make dolls out of different kinds of materials. She promised to make me a doll, and she made good on her promise. She made me this doll with a bonnet on her head and made her dress out of a green, printed, heavy material. On the face, she drew the eyes and nose and ears with what appeared to be black shoe polish. I kept that doll for years, until I married and moved to California. I named the doll after Mrs. James; I called her my "Rosie Doll."

In the late sixties, Mrs. James went to church one morning, and as she proceeded to kneel down to pray, her heart stopped. She was pronounced dead by the paramedics as she lay on the floor in church.

.

After the death of Mrs. James, her children married and moved away. One of her daughters remained in the house but who would later marry and start a family.

Early one morning in the early seventies, the house caught fire. Luckily the family escaped, but the house burned completely to the ground. After the lost of their house, this daughter and her husband constructed a larger, three-bedroom house on the property. They could have built a house anywhere, but they chose this site, because this place is sacred ground.

Chapter 10

Mr. & Mrs. Farris: The Survivors

Next door to the James family was the Farris family. This couple had eight children. They were considered financially well off. Mr. Farris was self-employed. He was a landscaper, and his wife did domestic work. One of their daughters was one of my best friends. We would play together after school until sundown. When the church attempted to raise money, the children in the community would knock on the neighbors' doors and ask for donations. We knew not to go to the Farris's house, because Mr. Farris refused to give. On one occasion, we were soliciting funds for our Sunday school and knocked on the Farris's door. Mr. Farris came to the door, and when we told him the purpose of our presence, he responded, "God never done anything for me." As the years passed, Mr. Farris would eventually have to come to know a much higher source because of what was about to happen in his life. In the early sixties, at approximately 4:00 a.m., the Farris household could be heard wailing throughout the community. They had received news their oldest son was killed in a car accident. I remember attending the funeral and viewing his body in the casket. What a remarkable resemblance. He looked just like his father; in fact, one could have mistaken him for Mr. Farris. Some years later, the fourth son apparently got into an altercation with another young male while attending a party on a Friday night. The young man shot Mr. and Mrs. Farris's son. The male and other companions brought Mr. and Mrs. Farris's son home, and they pushed his body out of the car. It was a very bitter, cold, winter night, and no one even bothered to get up to investigate the disturbance. The next day, one of the other siblings found his brother lying in the street directly in front of his house. He had remained there throughout the night, stiff as a board. He managed to bring him into the house and onto the bed, where the family gathered to grieve another loss. What a tragedy.

During the late sixties, the third son was drafted into the army. He served in Vietnam for nearly two years. He was blessed to survive the war and receive an honorable discharge. Yet, he would soon meet his fate. I would imagine the war played a significant impact on this son, because he began to drink alcohol excessively. During the early eighties, one of the nurses came out of the medical intensive care unit of a local Veterans Administration hospital, which was located within the ward where I was working. Her uniform was covered with blood. She explained that she had a bleeder. (This is a medical term that describes a condition in which an individual has large varicose veins in the esophagus that ruptures and causes one to hemorrhage to death.) This is a result of cirrhosis of the liver due to excessive alcohol consumption. Little did I know this was Mr. and Mrs. Farris's third son. Shortly after the nurse returned to the medical intensive care unit, I witnessed Mrs. Farris and her daughter, the one who was my best friend. They were being escorted to a waiting room to be consoled. Mrs. Farris was sobbing profusely, and her daughter was telling her, "Mom you knew this was going to happened." How helpless I felt. I wanted to go up to them, but they were embracing so tightly, as if to say, "This is our private moment." Approximately nine years after the death of this third son, the surviving son began to drink alcohol excessively. Perhaps the memories of losing three of his brothers were too much for him to handle, and he became dependent on alcohol. In fact, his drinking resulted in alcohol withdrawal seizures. In the summer of 1980, at approximately 1:00 p.m., sirens could be heard throughout our small community. Fire trucks and police cars came speeding by, passed through the main street, made a right turn and then another right, and parked directly in front of the Farris's house. I ran over to ask the neighbors already outside what had happened. They informed me that the fourth son had had a seizure and fallen in the bathroom, hitting his head; he died in the house. I reminisced about the death of the second son some years earlier, and how he was found shot dead in front of this same house. His body was found the following day by his brother. Again, the coroner was called to investigate the death of this fourth son, and the body had to lie in this same little, white-frame house pending the corner's investigation. Oh how awful. I immediately began to pray for the family, especially for Mrs. Farris, who had witnessed the death of four sons. Mrs. Farris was a soft-spoken, easygoing, churchgoing woman. Mrs. Farris showed great resiliency and faith after losing four sons. She continued to work daily and attended weekly church services. Mr. and Mrs. Farris and their youngest and only son were left to live in this small, frame house. As the years passed, their youngest son married and moved away, and Mr. and Mrs. Farris were alone. As time passed, Mr. Farris walked with the aid of a crutch. He had a noticeable weakness on one side of the body, so when he walked, his right foot would swing to the side as he walked. He became quite superstitious. He believed that a tall woman with a fair complexion had placed a curse on him. My aunt was a very tall woman with a fair complexion who lived with my grandmother on the same street where the Farrises lived. One summer day, while my grandmother and aunt were sitting on their front porch, Mr. Farris decided to take revenge. He got his gun and shot toward my grandmother's house. The target was, of course, my aunt. Luckily, his aim was off. Approximately ten years after the shooting incident occurred, I was working one Sunday morning at a local VA hospital. While I was bathing my patient, I happened to look up at the television. Someone was claiming to heal what appeared to be a multitude of people. Lo and behold, I witnessed Mr. Farris approach the healer, and he told him he had not been able to walk for years. The healer supposedly removed his crutch and proclaimed Mr. Farris to be healed that very moment! (Of course he maintained his weakness and dependency on a crutch.) I couldn't believe Mr. Farris had managed to travel two states to seek healing. Later, Mr. Farris received a tip that if he rubbed himself with gasoline, it would relieve him of his pain and help him to walk. One winter evening, he got some gasoline and began to rub it on himself in front of a space heater. In her gentle, sweet voice, Mrs. Farris cautioned Mr. Farris, "Honey, don't get too close to the heater with that gasoline." After Mrs. Farris exited the room, she heard a loud cry. When she reentered the room, she saw that her husband had ignited a fire and was engulfed in flames. Mrs. Farris called the emergency response team. When the team arrived, they treated him and transported him to the public hospital, where he later died as a result of his injuries. After the death of Mr. Farris, Mrs. Farris's young son and his family decided to move back to the community. He purchased land directly across the street from Mrs. Farris and later moved a trailer onto the site. I imagine the son's decision to move back pleased Mrs. Farris, as she now had her son and grandchildren directly across from her. Mrs. Farris continued to work, and I would see going to church on Sunday, wearing her wide-brim hat as she drove her small, white car. In fact, she appeared younger. Sometimes I would see her walking in tennis shoes and shorts to maintain her cardiovascular health and to remain physically fit. In 1999, I lost my mother, who was Mrs. Farris's age. In fact, they were once classmates. Mrs. Farris came to the wake, and she brought freshly cooked collard greens and soft drinks. I thought she must have known the grief I felt, since my mother and I lived together, and now I would have to live alone. After all, Mrs. Farris could have written a book on how to cope with grief. Years went by and Mrs. Farris's youngest son and his family decided to move, leaving her alone.

Months passed, and I noticed I hadn't seen Mrs. Farris for weeks. I asked a neighbor if she had seen Mrs. Farris. She informed me that Mrs. Farris had become ill and was hospitalized, and because she lived alone, she was placed in a nursing home. This must have been devastating to Mrs. Farris, who was once an independent, vibrant woman with all of her faculties. Now she had to live in a nursing facility. I kept promising myself I was going to visit her, because I remembered how thoughtful she was after the death of my mother. But one day I received news that

Mrs. Farris had died. I regretted that I never went to see her. In fact, I lived with a deep regret for quite some time. It was hard to accept the death of Mrs. Farris, because for months afterward, her car remained directly in front of her house, just as she had parked it. Eventually, the car was sold, and developers demolished the Farris's house and constructed a new, much larger house on the same cracked foundation. Today, although a new home has been constructed, I believe a deep spirit of the Farrises lives on this sacred ground.

Chapter 11

Grandpa/Grandma: Granpa/Grandma

My grandmother, grandfather, and aunt lived in a four-room house up the street from the Farrises. My aunt was a divorcee with two children, so the house was crowded. My grandmother could have been mistaken to be Caucasian. She had a very fair complexion, a very small waistline, broad hips, and silky, black, wavy hair. She was about five feet tall. I remember her thighs protruded as if she had a sandbag underneath her clothing. She had very high cheekbones, and she wore glasses. She was quite a disciplinarian. If she hit you, you really knew she meant business; you felt the blow over your entire body. She did domestic work and sometimes took in ironing for white people. My grandparents had seven children, all girls! My grandmother and grandfather never agreed on any issue. One Sunday, I witnessed my grandfather walking down the street talking to himself in an angry tone. He came to our house and told my mother that Grandmother had thrown the waste basket, striking him in the face. He vowed he would never again live with my grandmother. He made good on his word, because he never returned. He lived with us for a month prior to moving into a three-room duplex.

Grandpa was a very tall man: he stood over six feet tall. He, too, could have been mistaken to be white. He had thick, black hair and a very thick mustache. He almost always smoked a pipe and occasionally dipped snuff. He wore mostly coveralls with a long shirt. If the weather were hot, he would not wear any undergarment. As a result, when he sat in a chair, one could see his bare, white skin. Grandpa was a World War I veteran. During World War I, when African-Americans were promoted to higher ranks, they had no authority over white males of lower ranking. Additionally, when they were deployed to Europe, African men were not allowed to date French women. But I guess the military officers did not know Grandpa was an African-American, because he often told war stories of how he dated so many French women. He described the French women in one word: "Qui." He was quite unique, and most superstitious. For instance, regardless of how far he would walk in an attempt to reach a specific destination, if a black cat crossed his path from his right side, he would write an X on the ground, turn around, and return home. We never knew Grandpa's real age, because he said there were no recordings of his date of birth. Once, when my eldest brother accompanied him to sign up for Social Security benefits, one of the Social Security representatives asked him for his date of birth. Grandpa remained silent. The Social Security representative repeated the question. After a long period of silence, Grandpa finally responded in a loud voice, "How do I know? It was in the dark!" My grandfather was born in South Georgia, Green County. At one time, Green County was considered the poorest county in Georgia. He had a lot of cousins who remained in Green County, and it was important to Grandpa to keep in touch with his relatives. He would come to me and ask me to write letters for him. Grandfather was illiterate, and one would wonder how he was allowed to enlist into the army since he was unable to read or write. One day he dictated a letter to one of his cousins. After concluding writing the letter, I asked him to give me the street address. He responded, "Just put on there across the railroad track, below Mr. Dunn's house next to the old post office, the third house on the left of the road." I insisted I had to have a real address. He and I continued to argue until he exclaimed, "Blame fool, do what I tell you." I thought, This demented, old man wasted my time composing a letter that will never be delivered. But giving him respect, I addressed the envelope exactly the way he commanded. Amazingly, two weeks later, he returned with a letter in his hand. He had actually received a reply from his cousin! Perhaps the town was so small the postman knew everyone and their exact location. Moreover, the address on the envelope had so many landmarks that it was very easy to identify the addressee. Grandpa never used profanity. "Fool, "opossum," "old devil," "dat blame it" were the extinct of the adjectives he used in describing an individual or situation when he displayed anger. During one quarter at nursing school, I was studying the reproductive system. The page I was reading contained an illustration of the female organ. Grandpa looked over my shoulder and at the illustration of the female anatomy. I asked, "Grandpa, do you understand what you are looking at?" He looked at me in dismay. After a brief period of silence, he responded almost in a whispering tone, "Fool, you don't know what that is?" Grandpa was quite a character.

During my senior year in nursing school, my aunt asked me to go visit Grandpa. He was unable to walk and had been in bed, refusing to eat for nearly two weeks. I visited Grandpa one hot, summer day. He had three blankets on his bed and a bucket full of old urine and feces near the head of his bed. Apparently, he had become too weak to go to the outdoor toilet. He hated doctors, and he vowed never to go, because they would give you a shot, and, "Outside of six months, you will be dead." Yet, as a young child, I remember he spoke highly of doctors in a nearby town. So I convinced him to let me take him to see a doctor in that town (six miles from Atlanta). He got dressed. He could hardly walk, but I finally got him into my car. On arriving at the doctor's office, we found no seats available in the waiting room until one nice young man stood up and offered his chair. A young, blond, blue-eyed doctor, who looked no more than twenty-five at the most, came into the room where my grandfather and I were sitting. After taking Grandfather's blood pressure, he immediately ordered an injection of a diuretic to help lower his blood pressure. I didn't think Grandfather would let anyone give him an injection. I told him the injection would help him feel better. Shortly afterward, this young, attractive, dark-haired nurse entered the room to give Grandfather the shot. He looked up at her and, after a few seconds, managed to give her a smile. Perhaps Grandpa began to reflect on the time he was in France and the various Frenchwomen he encountered. Amazingly, he allowed the nurse to give him the injection. The doctor gave us a prescription and told grandfather to get it filled and to take the medication twice a day. Two months later, Grandpa's condition worsened. My aunt, who lived across the street, again called me and explained Grandpa had refused to take the medication. I convinced him to allow my uncle and me to take him to the hospital. I remembered Grandpa was a veteran, so I suggested to my uncle that we should take him to the local VA hospital. He was admitted and remained there for a month. Afterward, he was transferred to a local nursing facility, where he later died from renal failure. A vacant lot now exists where once upon a time there was the duplex where Grandpa lived. But my grandpa's spirit lives on. After all, this is sacred ground.

Chapter 12

Mr. & Mrs. Cato: A Marriage Made In Heaven

My family lived on the main street of this small community. The neighbors who lived in the second house (next door to Prune Face) were a couple who had ten children. Mr. and Mrs. Cato. All of Mr. and Mrs. Cato's children married, with the exception of the youngest son. Two of their grandchildren also lived with them. The two grandchildren were girls, with whom I played. These two girls were quite outspoken when it came to disrespecting the elderly. I would never even think of being disrespectful to my elders, because I would get the worst punishment imaginable. Mr. Cato worked for a local plumbing company. This was the era prior to modern technology. Mr. Cato would have to dig ditches all day, and at the end of the day, he would come home with his coveralls full of Georgia red clay. Mrs. Cato was a housewife. I remember how she would watch soap operas all day. Mr. and Mrs. Cato were very active in the community church. Ms. Cato worked diligently as a mother in the church, and Mr. Cato was one of the head deacons. When I was baptized at the community church, Mr. Cato was one of the two men who assisted the pastor during the baptism ceremony, which was held in a cement pool located outside on the church property. Years later, Mr. And Mrs. Cato's grandchildren and the youngest son married and moved away, leaving Mr. And Mrs. Cato alone. They were viewed as the most loving couple. Although Mr. Cato was up in his eighties, he drove Mrs. Cato to the market and church. Mr. Cato was a busy individual. For example, he maintained a vegetable garden of collard greens, turnips greens, tomatoes, and sweet potatoes. You almost never saw Mr. Cato idle. He kept busy either working in his garden, mowing his lawn, constructing a carport, or washing his car. If he became idle, he would think of something to do, such as making a device to secure the doors to his house or planting assorted flowers. He was a philosopher in own right. He couldn't read or write, but he was quite versed on world politics and knew biblical scriptures. I enjoyed visiting and talking to both of them. One day I stood out in the garden while Mr. Cato harvested some of his collard greens. He wanted to engage in a long conversation that day, to share his views on the condition of the world. One of thing he said I shall always remember: "You know, girl, this world is in bad shape. The only thing that's holding it together is the prayers of these old people, and when they leave this world, the world will be destroyed." Perhaps the news of the numerous local murders was a little too much for Mr. Cato to handle. Obviously, he was disturbed listening to the daily news. In January 1995, I paid the Catos a visit. During my visit, I asked how long they had been married. At that time, they told me they had been married for sixty-seven years! I thought this was quite extraordinary, especially when there was a high divorce rate. So I decided to contact the local newspaper to see if they could interview the Catos. When I spoke with an individual at the local newspaper, she exclaimed, "Perfect, we have been looking for an African-American couple that has been married for numerous years to feature in the paper during the week of Valentine." The local news reporter interviewed Mr. and Mrs. Cato, and their picture and an article were featured in the local paper. The article was titled "Marriages Made in Heaven." A Caucasian couple was also featured during that same week, and the articles were reversed. Mr. and Mrs. Cato's story was under the white couple, and vice versa. The newspaper apologized. As a result, Mr. and Mrs. Cato's picture and story were published in the local newspaper for two consecutive weeks! Four weeks after Mr. and Mrs. Cato were featured in the local paper, Mrs. Cato suffered a stroke, causing one of her arms to become paralyzed. After her stroke, Mrs. Cato could no longer perform such daily activities as cooking, bathing, and administering her daily dosage of insulin. One of her adult sons, who was divorced, moved in with Mr. and Mrs. Cato. She was happy to have her son back home, because he would cook for the two of them; sometimes he would serve her in bed. She marveled frequently over the fact her son had returned home, and she boasted about his superb culinary skills. This son found employment at a local business located on the same street where the Catos lived. He would prepare breakfast prior to leaving for work, and would return home on his lunch break to make their lunch. Mrs. Cato was recuperating remarkably well, and she was quite happy during this time. However, her elation would soon end.

One morning in September 1997, Mr. Cato noticed his son failed to get up to prepare breakfast as he did each morning. He entered his room to wake him, but he couldn't. The son had apparently died in his sleep. After Mr. Cato realized his son was dead, he entered Ms. Cato's bedroom, and in a calm voice, he touched her and said, "Mattie, Paul is dead." Mrs. Cato exclaimed, "What?" This was a great shock to both Mr. and Mrs. Cato, but especially to Mrs. Cato. She had lost this son on whom she had become so dependent. With his death, the Catos had lost five of their ten children. It would be months before Ms. Cato was back to herself. She was depressed. She talked continually how she missed this son, and she would reminisce the times when he prepared her meals. Mr. Cato became Mrs. Cato's primary caretaker after the death of their son. By this time, he was in his nineties. He attempted to take care of her to the best of his ability. He attended weekly worship service, but only occasionally; he was afraid to leave Mrs. Cato for a prolonged period of time. Their marriage was surely made in heaven. Two years after their son's death, Mr. Cato became ill. He had difficulties voiding. Based on his age and from patients I have known, I imagine he mostly likely had an enlarged prostate.

In September 1999, Mr. Cato died. Mrs. Cato was heartbroken; she admitted she did not know the severity of her husband's illness. Unfortunately, I was out of town during the funeral of Mr. Cato, but I wrote a tribute to him to be read at his funeral. I reflected on his generosity, how he would plant turnips for me, and how he harvested and washed them for me after I had undergone surgery. In 2000, Mrs. Cato became ill and had to undergo abdominal surgery. She developed complications after the surgery and died at the same hospital where Mr. Cato had died a year earlier. Although the Cato's house was brought by an investor and refurbished, the house's structure remains basically the same as when the Catos lived there. The room where their son died and the vacant lot where Mr. Cato planted his garden stand as reminders of the Catos' lives. For years after the death of Mr. Cato, patches of turnips appeared in the garden during the fall. After all, this is sacred ground.

Chapter 13

Mr. & Mrs. Jenkins: The Bedrock

Mr. and Mrs. Jenkins lived adjacent to Mr. and Mrs. Cato. Mr. Jenkins wore his naturally thick, curly hair slicked back, and he kept very long sideburns. He had a mouth full of gold teeth They were a well-respected couple with two children, a boy and a girl. Mr. Jenkins was a very tall, distinguished-looking man, who stood approximately six and one-half feet tall. He had the most beautiful bronze complexion and very high cheekbones. In fact, he may have had Cherokee in his bloodline. Then, on the other hand, because of his height and facial features, he reminded you of President Abraham Lincoln. Mr. Jenkins was an entrepreneur and a landscaper; Mrs. Jenkins did domestic work at a local university.

On Sundays, he could be seen wearing his high-top, wide-brim hat.

He usually wore a freshly cut flower in his lapel. The flowers were handpicked from his flower garden. He had the most beautifully manicured lawn, with many assorted flowers. He sculpted his scrubs in the shapes of animals such as ducks, chickens, and elephants, just like the shrubs at Disney World. Motorists would often stop to get a glimpse of Mr. Jenkins's beautiful lawn and flower garden. His yard was simply breathtaking. Petunias, tulips of various colors, and begonias arranged in perfect order could be seen for blocks. A sculpted deer was placed in the front, and a gazebo stood to the right side of his front lawn. Mr. Jenkins purchased grass seed from Florida when he deemed necessary to maintain his beautiful hunter's green lawn. As a result, his lawn was at least three inches thick and manicured to perfection. To add to this beautiful lawn, Mr. Jenkins added customized signs containing biblical phrases in front of his yard. They challenged motorists to think about whether heaven or hell would be their destiny. One sign asked," Are you saved?" The next line read, "Be Very Sure." Mr. Jenkins had two large stones transported from a rock quarry. These stones were placed at the entrance of his driveway and painted with the words, "On This Rock I Build My Church." In addition to have a beautiful lawn, Mr. Jenkins had a very productive food garden. During the summer, you could see rows of corn and tomatoes. During the fall, one could find collard greens and turnip greens on the acre of land adjacent to his property.

Mrs. Jenkins worked daily until she reached retirement. Although she could not officially be called an entrepreneur, one could call her a wise investor. She took every opportunity to save a percentage of her earnings by purchasing U.S. Saving Bonds, certificates of deposit (certificate deposits were introduced during the latter years of her employment), and making deposits into a regular savings account.

Mrs. Jenkins also advised children in the community to invest in their future by saving rather than shopping frivolously.

Mr. and Mrs. Jenkins's house was on a half-acre of land, large enough for two houses. Mr. and Mrs. Jemkin's son, daughter-in-law, and grandchildren lived next door. They lived in a wooden-frame house that had a tin roof. Living next door was convenient for this teenage son and his wife, because Mrs. Jenkins could assist in preparing meals whenever her daughter-in-law was unable to cook, especially after giving birth. In the mid-fifties, her son and daughter-in-law had four children, including a set of twins. Mrs. Jenkins's son dropped out of school; he found it was lucrative to work with his father. Each day they would landscape yards that were miles away. They would work from sunup, and sometimes they would not return home until nightfall. Mr. Jenkins, his son, and hired workers would start their day by gearing up oversized trucks and tractors. The large engines could be heard over the entire community. Mrs. Jenkins would depart shortly afterward to report to work at a local university, where she did domestic work. Mrs. Jenkins never learned to drive, so she carpooled with a neighbor who worked at the same university. This neighbor whom she rode would begin blowing her horn for blocks. This was unnecessary, because Mrs. Jenkins would be standing at the edge of her driveway, waiting for her neighbor to arrive. After a long day's work, Mrs. Jenkins would prepare a nutritious dinner. She would cook fresh vegetables from her garden, making sure there was enough food in the event her son and his family wanted to eat. During the summer months, when we would play near the Jenkins's residence, we could smell the lemon cake baking for blocks, not to mention the vegetables cooked with green onions. The aroma would heighten anyone's appetite. Even today, the smell of cooked onions and freshly bake cake remind me of the Jenkins household. Mrs. Jenkins should have entered a cooking contest, especially for her lemon pound cakes. I have tasted many Southern, home-baked pound cakes, but during my entire life, none of the cakes I have eaten could surpass Mrs. Jenkins's!

Compared to the average family in the nation in the sixties, Mr. and Mrs. Jenkins would be considered economically upper middle class. Life couldn't have been better. Mr. and Mrs. Jenkins's daughter was preparing to enroll in college. This was major for this small community, because she would be the first in the community to attend college! Mr.

Jenkins drove a large Cadillac with encryption of the Twenty-Third Psalm, "The Lord is my Shepherd." These were most exciting times for the Jenkins family. But nothing could have prepared them for what was about to occur that would change their lives forever.

One winter morning, Mr. Jenkins and his son went to work as usual. and Mrs. Jenkins's neighbor picked her up, and they proceeded to work as they did daily. Mrs. Jenkins's daughter-in law was a homemaker and remained at home to take care of the children. This particular morning, Mrs. Jenkins' daughter-in-law stepped into the kitchen to take care of chores while the children played. On completing her chores and before she reentered the room, the house was engulfed in flames. One of the twins (the female) was severely burned by a fire that started from a coal-burning stove. The other twin was unscathed. When the firefighters arrived, they began evacuation and provided emergency treatment to the twin in preparation of transporting her to the local public hospital. The house burned to the ground. The twin died as a result of the burns she sustained. I was very young and attended the funeral as a flower girl. I didn't understand why this little girl had to die. I remember seeing her and her twin walking hand in hand as they passed my house. Understandably, this tragic event was very hard for the Jenkins family, but their faith in God sustained them, and they managed to carry on with their lives.

Mr. and Mrs. Jenkins did remarkably well in view of losing their granddaughter. The household went on to experience many proud moments. For example, Mr. and Mrs. Jenkins's daughter graduated from college and became a teacher. She would later marry and begin her own family. Mr. and Mrs. Jenkins demolished their old small house and constructed a much larger, three-bedroom, beautiful, pink, brick home. They moved a large, white, frame home onto the back of their property for their son and his family. This large home was much needed, because their son and daughter-in-law now had a total of seven children. Amazingly, two of the seven children were twins, two boys. Can you imagine? This was their second set of twins.

Later, as years passed, Mr. and Mrs. Jenkins's seven grandchildren finished high school, married, and pursued various careers. One of the twin boys enlisted in the U.S. Army. The twin who enlisted in the army received an honorable discharge and returned home. The twins were once again united. Yet, this would be short-lived. The Jenkins family was about to encounter another challenging event. Once again, their faith would be tested.

The twin who had enlisted and returned from the army tested positive for HIV. Shortly afterward, he was diagnosed with AIDS. This was in the early nineties, and pharmacological treatment methods were not as advanced as today. Today, we have extensive research, and there are clinical trials. Individuals who test positive for HIV are living longer without going into full-blown AIDS. But this twin would go into full-blown AIDS and succumb to this dreadful disease. How tragic this was for Mr. and Mrs. Jenkins to lose a second grandchild, not to mention the effect it had on their son and his wife. (Years later they would divorce). You would think this would have taken a toll on Mr. and Mrs. Jenkins, but their deeply rooted faith in God kept them strong, as did the community prayed for them vehemently. Mr. and Mrs. Jenkins helped their son and daughter-in-law make funeral arrangements for their second child. Mr. Jenkins owned one of the two cemeteries located in the community, so the burial plot was already slated.

The funeral was very beautiful. Because this grandson was a veteran, he was buried in his military uniform. On arriving at the funeral home chapel to view the body, I couldn't help but notice a young Caucasian male staring at the body in the casket. I could see how deeply affected he was. He would cry out intermittently and later remark how good he looked and how he would miss him. Weeks after the funeral, Mr. and Mrs. Jenkins attempted to continue their routine, but understandably, this loss affected them deeply. I noticed they would have their floodlights on at 4:00 a.m. Mrs. Jenkins would walk to the mailbox, but very slowly. The community continued to pray. But unfortunately, the Jenkins's grieving would be extended, because they were about to be confronted with another tragedy. Approximately two months after the death of Mr. and Mrs. Jenkins's grandson, his surviving twin became ill. He was admitted into the hospital with a fever and flu-like symptoms. The physician diagnosed him with AIDS. Mrs. Jenkins's daughter-in-law brought him home and was his primary caretaker. Although Mrs. Jenkins was warned not to have direct contact with her grandson, she refused to listen. She insisted she was going to help her daughter-in-law take care of him. After losing two grandchildren, she was determined to do all she could for this grandson, whose prognosis was grave. As the grandson's condition worsened, he became unable to control his bowels and bladder. As a result, he had to wear adult diapers. Mrs. Jenkins would change her grandson's soiled linens, and she would cook and attempt to feed him. She walked back and forth from her house many times every day to check on him. The grandson was transported to the hospital frequently, especially when he spiked a fever or became dehydrated because of his inability to swallow. It was common to see the emergency response team pull into the Jenkins's driveway and proceed to the son's house to transport the grandson to the hospital. In October 1993, the grandson was hospitalized like so many previous hospital admissions. But this time would be different: he would never return home. This grandson, one of the second sets of twins, died approximately eight months after the death of his twin brother. Mr. and Mrs. Jenkins experienced the death of three grandchildren, two within eight months apart! The parents, although divorced, were united, they grieved deeply .

Three months passed after Mr. and Mrs. Jenkins lost their grandson. After this latest tragedy, Mr. and Mrs. Jenkins continued to attend weekly church services, and they were putting their life back together as best they could. On Christmas Eve 1993, Mrs. Jenkins, as usual, was baking Christmas cakes. Suddenly, Mr. Jenkins fell off the chair at the kitchen table, where he had been eating. Mrs. Jenkins was horrified. She phoned 911, and the emergency response team transported him to the local hospital. On examination, he was diagnosed as having suffered a stroke, which left him paralyzed and slightly aphasic (unable to speak). Mr. Jenkins remained in the hospital for nearly five weeks of acute care followed by rehabilitation. Subsequently, he was discharged home. Mrs. Jenkins was physically unable to lift or take care of Mr. Jenkins. The niece, daughter-in-law, and grandchildren assisted in caring for him. This once-proud independent man would have never dreamed of becoming dependent on others to bathe him and to take care of his daily hygiene. He could be heard praying for the Lord to take him home. Approximately three weeks after he was discharged from the hospital, Mr. Jenkins's niece came as she always did each day to bathe him. This particular morning, however, was quite different. He did not fight her when she began to bathe him. Later that day, four months after the death of the second grandson, Mr. Jenkins died. How devastating this was for Mrs. Jenkins, as she was now left to live alone and with the memory of her husband dying in the home.

After the death of her husband, Mrs. Jenkins attempted to pick up the pieces in spite of the many personal losses she had encountered. She would attend church, but not as often, and she would walk very slowly. She and my mother would have daily phone conversations about various topics, but the number-one subject they shared was how they both missed their husbands and what they would do if they could have them back in their lives (my father had been deceased for thirty-years at this time). They often joked about this in their daily conversations. I recall my conversations with Mr. Jenkins, especially one. I remember vividly it was his desire to rename the name of the street in our community to a more worthy name. The street was named after a nearby town that had a negative reputation. This nearby town was known for violent acts, such as numerous murders, and its high percentage of high school dropouts. Although it was a year and half since the death of Mr. Jenkins, I wanted to do two things: pay homage to Mr. Jenkins and lift Mrs. Jenkins's spirit by spearheading a petition to rename the name of our street to Jenkins Lane. I presented my proposal to three branches of county government. After being confronted with opposition, and yet having the support from other local citizens, the street was renamed one year after the death of Mr. Jenkins. A ribbon-cutting ceremony was held, and the county commissioners were invited. We had music and barbeque for the entire community. The local news media was also invited, but they did not attend; perhaps the event was too small. A week after the ribbon-cutting ceremony, Mrs. Jenkins fell, bruising herself but fortunately, did not sustain any broken bones. She continued to fall, until the grandchildren and nieces noticed bruises over her body. One day she fell, but this time she fractured her hip. Since she lived alone, her daughter paid sitters to care for her. Mrs. Jenkins never fully recovered after sustaining the fractured hip. She died approximately seven years after the death of Mr. Jenkins. Mr. and Mrs. Jenkins's house was sold to an investor, the beautiful shrubs are no longer sculptured in the shapes of animals, the grass is no longer manicured to perfection, and there are no more petunias and begonias. The son remarried and the daughter-inlaw moved to a local city. The house remains empty in the back of the parcel and needs major repairs. It brings back so many memories to see the site where the Jenkins family once lived. Yet, Mr. and Mrs. Jenkins's spirit lives on this sacred ground.

Chapter 14

Mr. & Mrs. Meyers: The Newborn Child

Mr. and Mrs. Meyers lived directly across the street from the Jenkins family. They were unable to have children. Mrs. Meyers often talked about her desire to have a son, so when she was in her late forties, Mr. and Mrs. Meyers adopted a newborn son. Mrs. Meyers was the talk of this small community. The neighbors said she was too old to take care of a child. She depended on the neighbors for advice when the infant had a cold, and about how much food to give the baby. She also consulted neighbors on how to change the infant's diaper. But over time, Mrs. Meyers proved to be the best mother this child could have ever had. Mr. Meyers, like Mrs. Meyers, loved his son and was a very proud father. He would purchase son anything he thought he needed—and almost everything he asked for. At Christmas, there would be so many toys in the Meyers's house that it looked like a toy store! The child's genuine love for his parents, the only ones he had ever known, would be tested. You see, Mr. and Mrs. Meyers never told their son he was adopted and that his biological mother became pregnant while attending college. She wanted to graduate from college, so she gave him up for adoption. However, years later, after she graduated from college, the biological mother phoned Mrs. Meyers one morning. She expressed how badly she wanted to see her child and the desire to have him come back to live with her. Mrs. Meyer's heart was broken. One summer day she came to tell my mother about the call she had received and how afraid she was that she was going to lose her only child, whom she had since birth. My mom consoled her by telling her that everything would be all right and she would not lose her child. Weeks after Mrs. Meyers received the phone call from the biological mother, the woman could be seen parked near the bus stop where the school bus dropped off all the children in the community. Mrs. Meyers stood waiting each afternoon to make sure the biological mother did not kidnap her child. The thought of losing her only child worried her so much that Mr. and Mrs. Meyers decided to tell their son the truth about his adoption and that his biological mother wanted him back. The child became furious! He cried and told Mr. and Mrs. Meyers that he never known anyone but the two of them, and they were the only mother and father he had ever known. Even at eight years old, the child was bright, and he genuinely loved his adopted parents as if they were his biological parents. He assured them both that he was not going to leave them and that he would talk to his biological mother if she ever returned. Months passed, and one day his biological mother was again parked near the bus stop. Mr. and Mrs. Meyers's son was on the lookout for a strange individual parked nearby. So he went to his biological mother and told her he did not know her, and the only parents he had were Mr. and Mrs. Meyers. He told her to leave and never return, because he did not need her. The biological mother never returned.

Mrs. Meyers was approximately six feet tall and weighed about three hundred pounds. She had very high cheekbones. On Sundays, she wore the largest and most exotic hats to church. She would drive way beyond the speed limit to make sure she arrived on time to church. As children, we tried to avoid sitting next to Mrs. Meyers during worship service. Invariably, when the spirit came upon her, her arms would extend, and the persons sitting on either side of her would surely get their faces slapped. It would take three and sometimes four men to contain her. First, her hat would land on the floor, then her dress would go up, and her nice French roll hairdo would come undone. By the time the worship service was over, Mrs. Meyers looked as if she had been in a brawl. Of course, the short, small-framed deacons did not fare much better. Sometimes their suit coats would be twisted, their buttons missing, and their shirts untucked.

Mrs. Meyers did domestic work until she was beyond her seventies. She was the most compassionate individual I have ever known. Each Christmas, she would go to each neighbor's door to deliver them slices of cakes. She had labored over a hot stove the night before in a house that did not have air conditioning and was infested with termites. Every Christmas morning, my family expected Mrs. Meyers to knock on our door. On opening the door, Mrs. Myers, with a large smile, would be standing there holding a large platter of slices of assorted cakes. They included chocolate, coconut, butterscotch, lemon pound, and fruit cakes that she had prepared for weeks in advance. Mr. Meyers was also a very tall and overweight. He stood about six and one-half feet tall and weighed approximately three hundred pounds. He had solid white hair for as long as I remember, with long, white sideburns and very thick eyebrows. The children in the community nicknamed him "Uncle Ramos." He was a quiet, well-mannered, easygoing man who horded a lot of cars on his parcel. He worked as a horseman. As a horseman, his primary responsibility was to groom and feed the horses, and to ensure they made a good showing during horse shows. Mr. and Mrs. Meyers worked for the same employer. While Mrs. Meyers did maid work inside the compounds, Mr. Meyers worked outside, grooming and picking up the horses' fecal droppings. This employer thought well of the two of them. On their employer's death, in his last will and testament, the employer left Mr. and Ms. Meyers a total of $40,000, $20,000 each. Because of this inheritance, Mr. and Mrs. Meyers built a very large, four-bedrooms house on their parcel. Mrs. Meyers always dreamed of having a new home. Once the new house was completed, the Meyerses moved in it debt free! This was a very generous gift, but I am sure they deserved even more. Once, after Mrs. Meyers had completed a day's work, she visited my mother and told how her boss had made racial remarks. Yet, Mrs. Meyers tried to tell her about spirit of the Lord and what a difference He had made in her life. Mrs. Meyers said the employer refused to listen. Mrs. Meyers loved her new home. The house was two stories because the property was very narrow, so the house was vertically constructed. It was perplexing to see Mrs. Meyers sitting on the front porch on an unusually hot summer day, especially since she had central heating and air in her new home. Perhaps Mrs. Meyers could not break the old habit of sitting on her porch, or perhaps being inside was too remote. After Mrs. Meyers moved into her new home, you could see a change in her demeanor. She didn't attend church as often as before, and she would stay to herself. Sometimes she would call me to come down to take her blood pressure when she felt ill. She began to visit the doctor's office more regularly. One day while I was visiting her, she complained of pin-like sensation in both her arms. I advised her to get a doctor's appointment the following day. Weeks passed, and I noticed Mrs. Meyers was not sitting on her front porch. I later learned she had a stroke and was hospitalized. Mrs. Meyers was later placed in a nursing home, since her husband, who was up in age, could not take care of her. The nursing facility was less than a mile from her home, so Mr. Meyers would drive each afternoon to visit her. Once when I visited at the nursing facility, the nurses commented to me when I asked if I might visit Mrs. Meyers, "Oh you want to see Mrs. Meyers, the woman who is always singing gospel songs." During Mrs. Meyers's stay in the nursing facility, she had to wear diapers. Sometimes she refused to allow the nurses to change her diapers; yet with the exception of one individual, her son. Her son could do more for her sometimes than the nurses. The mother–son roles were reversed from those earlier years, when Mrs. Meyers longed for a child and cared for her son. Approximately six months after being placed in the nursing home, Mrs. Meyers died. Mr. Meyers is now in his eighties. He is frail and has cataracts. His son, although married, cares for him with the assistance of one of the neighbors. Mr. and Mrs. Meyer's first house—where Mrs. Meyers stood over a hot stove baking cakes for the community at Christmas, the house infested with termites, and most of all, the house that was filled with love—has been torn down. The only thing left to remind us the house was once there is the large oak tree that once that stood over the now-gone house. Mrs. Meyers's memories live on this site, because this is sacred ground.

Chapter 15

The Lawson Family: The Dream

Next door to Mr. and Mrs. Meyers was the Lawson family, who rented a small, three-bedroom, frame house from the Meyerses. Mr. and Mrs. Lawson had seventeen children but they separated years earlier. All were grown and had moved away, with the exception of one daughter who never married but had a daughter. The daughter never lived anywhere but in this small community with her mother. Her mother divorced her husband years earlier, so there were three who made up the Lawson's household: Mrs. Lawson (the mother), Miss Lawson (the daughter), and the granddaughter.

Mrs. Lawson was a very quiet, sweet, short woman with a very beautiful golden-brown complexion. She wore cotton dresses and an apron. She would often be seen wearing a scarf tied around her head as she worked in her small vegetable garden. Sundays she attended the worship service dressed in a white uniform and gloves white as snow. She served on the Mother Board at the community church. She was an excellent cook. She would bake fresh coconut cakes, grating her coconut from a fresh coconut. The cake would be so moist it would melt in your mouth. Mrs. Lawson's daughter did domestic work. Her employer she worked for picked up the daughter every day. As economic conditions worsened, they reduced the daughter's wages by reducing her services to three times a week. The Lawson household was one of faith. The family was deeply rooted in their Christian belief. They didn't believe in gossiping about anyone, and they were basically a private family. Moreover, the Lawsons did not want others meddling in their personal affairs. No one ever knew who the granddaughter's father was, and no one dared to asked. Miss Lawson, the daughter, wanted the best for her only child. She would often talk about sending her child to college, and in return, her daughter would buy her a house. Miss Lawson indeed gave her only child the best. On Easter Sundays, my new dress could not be compared to Miss Lawson's daughter's dress. Miss Lawson's daughter's brightly colored dress stood up when she sat down, because many starch slips were attached to it. Additionally, she would have matching gloves and hat, not to mention the purse and the beautiful lace socks and patent shoes. Her hairdo was as if she had gone to a stylist. As the years passed,

Miss Lawson's daughter graduated from business college and shortly afterward, moved out and married. Miss Lawson's dreams of moving away from this small community and into a dream house dissipated. Yet, she helped planned her daughter's wedding, and she began to view the positive aspect of the marriage: she was gaining not only a son-in-law but a son as well. During late eighties, the Lawson household was about to undergo challenges that would affect the family. Mrs. Lawson, who was up in her nineties, became frail and weak. She became less mobile and had to walk with an assistance device. One Sunday evening in the early seventies, the Lawsons phoned me and asked if I would go to Mrs. Lawson's home to take her blood pressure because she had become ill. On arrival, Mrs. Lawson was sitting on a sofa in the front room. The room had pine paneling on the walls and numerous pictures of the granddaughter—from a very young age to her enlisting in Job Corp., high school graduation, and then graduation from business college. Looking back, this granddaughter/daughter was their pride and joy and for whom they had had such high aspirations. Obviously, they were very proud of her because, at that time, she had achieved more than anyone else in the Lawson's family.

Sitting next to Mrs. Lawson, I asked her to describe how she was feeling. She described how she felt weak and that she was experiencing pain in both arms. I took her blood pressure, and although it was not exceedingly elevated, as a nurse, I knew that a stroke could not be ruled out. I had learned from working with people who had experienced a stroke that blood pressure is not always elevated immediately after the stroke. I sat with her and tried to keep her calm. I began to tell her how my father (who was deceased) thought the world of her, and she expressed how she admired my father. I continued to hold her hand while we conversed. Meanwhile, the paramedics had been called. As we sat there, the granddaughters arrived. Once they entered the room, I informed Mrs. Lawson I would be leaving. She responded, "You don't have to go." I had gained her complete trust. Soon the paramedics came and transported her to the hospital. Months later, Mrs. Lawson died. Miss Lawson now was left to live alone, since her only child had married and relocated. Her daughter and husband often visited her on Sundays and holidays. Miss Lawson lived alone until her two adult brothers eventually returned to live with her in the small, wooden-frame house. These two brothers had very different lifestyles compared to Miss Lawson's. For example, neither of the brothers attended church, they liked to drink beer with their comrades, and they smoked and stayed up late at night. These were pretty tumultuous times for Miss Lawson. As the years went by, Miss Lawson, as usual, had an annual mammography. However, the result was unfavorable. She was diagnosed with breast cancer, and the physician recommended that she undergo surgery (mastectomy). Subsequently, Miss Lawson had the surgery and she recuperated well postoperatively. In fact, in a few months she returned to weekly church services. She maintained her doctor's appointments for follow-up examinations. All of the examinations revealed she was cancer free. Yet, she would soon get another report, this one unfavorable. What was about to happen would change her life forever. In the early nineties, Miss Lawson's only child became ill. She, too, was diagnosed with breast cancer. But her cancer had metastasized to other vital organs. The daughter would have to undergo radiation therapy and chemotherapy, but no surgery since this was considered end-stage. The daughter needed close monitoring to ensure she ate and drank plenty of liquids since she was undergoing chemotherapy. The daughter's husband could not take care of her. Miss Lawson's daughter returned home so her mother could care for her, just as she had always done. The daughter's physical features were altered. Radiation had taken a toll on the daughter's complexion. Once the most beautiful golden brown, just like her grandmother's, the daughter's complexion had been turned very dark by the treatment. Moreover, her facial features had changed until she was unrecognizable. Miss Lawson attempted to take care of her daughter, making sure she received treatments. Since the Lawsons were a private family, Miss Lawson did not tell the church or anyone in the community of her daughter's illness until later, when one could not help but notice the daughter's physical transformation. One summer morning in 1998, Miss Lawson heard her daughter in the next bedroom make a grunting sound. She tried to arouse her daughter, but she could not be awaken. Miss Lawson's daughter died in the small house where she, her mother, and grandmother had lived for so many years. Mrs. Lawson made funeral arrangements with the help of her nieces and her daughter's high school classmates. The funeral was very sad. Miss Lawson cried out continually, "I did the best I could do," as she continued to cry soberly. Weeks passed, and Miss Lawson continued to grieve. Although she tried to attend weekly services, I noticed how slowly she would walk to the community church with her sister, who was also a member of the church. Miss Lawson kept busy in the church. She was president of the Usher Board, the position she held nearly all of her adult life. Apparently, she was either voted into this office at every election, or no one would ever dream of challenging her by running against her. She would call biweekly meetings even when there was no reason to hold such meetings. Perhaps these meetings were therapeutic for Miss Lawson. However, after the members complained, the meetings were rescheduled to occur monthly.

In 2004, Miss Lawson complained of severe arm and back pain. The pain became so excruciating Miss Lawson was unable to attend weekly services. She would attend every other Sunday, which was most unusual. Later she obtained a doctor's appointment. The physician decided to perform extensive radiological examinations. The tests confirmed the cancer had metastasized to the bone. Miss Lawson was now living alone, because she had evicted her two older brothers because of their different lifestyles. She would have to undergo weeks of radiation therapy, and she would need someone to transport her back and forth to the radiation center. She would also need someone to take care of her when she was unable to eat, or when she got sick at night. Her sister, who lived around the corner, would visit with her during the day. As time went on, she had to bathe her and assist in feeding her. These two sisters were estranged. Although Miss Lawson and her sister lived in the same community, Miss Lawson never visited her sister, no matter how many times her sister invited her to come visit. But Miss Lawson's illness brought these two sisters together. As time went on and Miss Lawson's condition worsened, she begged her sister to spend the night. The sister instead pleaded with her to move in with her, so she could attend to her twenty-four hours a day. Miss Lawson refused. Miss Lawson decided to move in with one of her elderly brothers, and that is where she later died.

Today, the Lawson's house is vacant, ready to be demolished. The same kitchen curtains Mrs. Lawson hung on the kitchen door can be still be seen. The screened porch is nearly collapsing, supported mainly by cement blocks. The screen enclosing the front porch is nearly completely off, and some of the windows are shattered. The gardenia bush along the small, gravel driveway has almost always been trimmed. Now it has grown as tall as the roof of the house. The house is empty, but the spirit of the Lawsons continues to linger on this sacred ground.

Chapter 16

Mr. & Mrs. Clark: The Teacher/Singer

Mr. and Mrs. Clark lived across the street from the Lawsons. Mr. and Mrs. Clark had five children, three boys and two girls. Mr. and Mrs. Clark were very active in the community church. Mr. Clark was once the superintendent of the Sunday school. On Sundays, he would dress in a three-piece suit, and he almost always had a fanciful walking cane; look out Freddie Stare! Mrs. Clark was most active in the church choir. When the church observed an anniversary or some special event, various guest choirs would be invited. We couldn't wait until it was our choir's turn to sing. Mrs. Clark led most of the songs. She could hit those high notes and put Whitney Houston to shame. Her voice was so electrifying it was almost impossible for anyone sitting in the audience to sit without patting their foot or clapping their hands. Mr. and Mrs. Clark were petite. Mr. Clark appeared to be 5'10" tall and weighed about 160 pounds. Mrs. Clark was approximately 5' tall and she weighed about 100 pounds. She had a very small waistline; I would say probably an eighteen-inch waistline. She would accentuate her waist by wearing wide belts of various colors. Mr. Clark's mother, who appeared to be over a hundred years old, lived in the house next to Mr. and Mrs. Clark. I remember she had a very fair complexion and a large mole on her nose. She could have been mistaken for Caucasian. As the years went by, Mr. Clark's mother expired, and her house was torn down. Mr. Clark died of natural causes, and Mrs. Clark lived nearly thirty years after the death of her husband. She became quite ill. Her daughter, who never married, became her primary caretaker. Today, the daughter lives alone in the same small home. This is sacred ground.

Chapter 17

Mr. & Mrs. Barnes: The Devoted Couple

Mr. and Mrs. Barnes worked as domestic workers at a nearby college. In fact, this was the same college where I attended nursing school. As I walked on campus I would frequently run into the two of them working side by side as a team. They would marvel over the fact I was enrolled in a predominately white college. This was the very early sixties after all. Mr. and Mrs. Barnes had eight children, four boys and four girls. Mr. Barnes was apparently the disciplinarian of the two, because the children would make every effort to do their chores or face the punishment of their father. Mr. Barnes was a very tall man, over six feet tall, but with a very small frame. He had a very pronounced Southern drawl. As children, we would imitate the manner in which he spoke. Mrs. Barnes was also tall; she was almost six feet tall. Mr. and Mrs. Barnes were very active in the community church. Mr. Barnes was a deacon, and Mrs. Barnes was a member on the Mother Board.

After graduating from high school, the Barnes's children married and moved away, with the exception of one daughter. Mr. and Mrs. Barnes were retired, and their life couldn't have been better. But this was only temporary. Mr. Barnes became ill. The doctor ordered a series of diagnostic tests that revealed Mr. Barnes had prostate cancer. After Mr. Barnes was diagnosed with prostate cancer, the Barneses had to adjust their lives. Mr. Barnes became confined to a wheelchair. A ramp was installed at the entrance to their house so Mr. Barnes could go back and forth for his medical treatments. Mr. Barnes eventually succumbed to his cancer, leaving Mrs. Barnes and her daughter. Mrs. Barnes's youngest son moved back home. Now Mrs. Barnes had two of her children living with her. I imagine this pleased her, since she had her oldest daughter and her youngest son. One day the son asked to borrow Ms. Barnes's car, and on exiting into the main street, a car struck him. His automobile was thrown approximately twenty-five feet into an embankment. Fortunately, he was not injured, but the car was a total loss. Mrs. Barnes was quite affected by the lost of her car. When she received her monthly retirement check each month, she would drive herself to the bank do her monthly shopping. Now she was dependent on others. But this would not be Mrs. Barnes's only loss. One summer day in the mid-nineties, her son, who had visited neighbors in the community, fainted suddenly.

The neighbor called the emergency response, but on arrival to the hospital, Mrs. Barnes's youngest son died. Mrs. Barnes was never the same. She grieved continually, talking often about how she missed her son. She tried to continue to live, but it was most taxing. She decided she needed a car, so she purchased a brand-new, metallic gray Buick. (Her former car was a Buick.) Once again, Mrs. Barnes began driving back and forth to the market and to church each Sunday. But losing her youngest son was too much for her to handle. She often experienced shortness of breath until she would have to be admitted to the hospital every other month. Sometimes, she would remain in the hospital three to four weeks at a time. Her breathing became so severe she became dependent on supplemental oxygen.

In spite of Mrs. Barnes's medical condition, she continued to support any endeavors to improve the community. She would attend community meetings and assisted in any way possible. In 2006, Mrs. Barnes continued to experience difficulty breathing. She was admitted to the hospital, but unlike the previous hospital admissions, she would never return home. Mrs. Barnes died in the hospital. Today, Mrs. Barnes's small house, embellished with awnings on each window and an enclosed screened porch, is a reminder that this house was where Mr. and Mrs. Barnes raised their children. The hanging baskets remain dangling over the front porch, and the pottery that once contained an assortment of flowers gives a false perception that Mrs. Barnes is still alive because this is the manner in which she arranged the hanging floral baskets. Yet, Mr. and Mrs. Barnes are no longer physically present. Their spirit continues to live on this sacred ground.

Chapter 18

Mr. & Mrs. Eason: The Preacher

Mr. and Mrs. Eason lived two houses down the street from the Barnes.

Mr. Eason was relatively short; he was approximately 5'11" tall. Mrs. Eason was much taller, about 5'6" tall. She was from the Florida Keys, so she had a very pronounced accent. When she spoke, she would pronounce each syllable. For that reason, she got people's attention whenever she spoke. She was a very kindhearted, soft-spoken woman. Back in the fifties, homeschooling was not heard of. However, Mrs. Eason played a vital role in ensuring each of her children was educated. She did not only teach them, but she would monitor each child's homework each day. Moreover, she was active in the church. She coordinated the Easter program and was the youth choir director. Additionally, she traveled with her husband, visiting churches when he was called on to preach. So, although she did not work in a job for a major corporation, she probably worked harder than most of her neighbors who worked a regular eight-hour job. Indeed, she was an amazing woman who was respected by most in the community. Mr. Eason was considered the leader of the community. He earned this title because he was the minister of the community church. During the week, he performed janitorial services at a local university, and on Sundays, he could be found preaching in the pulpit at the small, white, wooden-frame church. Mr. Eason lived strictly by the Old Testament of the Bible. He believed that in a marriage, the man should be the head of the household; the woman's responsibility was to take care of the daily household tasks. Mrs. Eason, although a college graduate, never worked outside the home because of Mr. Eason's belief. Mr. Eason's Sundays sermons were filled with fire and brimstone. He knew the Bible better than some theologians did. Though he never attended any theology school, over years of studying, he became one of the most effective ministers in the county. Women were not allowed to wear wearing pants to church And d uring the worship service, unless you were an ordained minister, you could not come up on the pulpit to speak. During the late fifties, the church did not have central heating. The church had a wooden heater that sat in the middle of the church. So when weekly Bible study was held in the evenings, Mr. Eason would get there early to begin heating the church. Frequently, just one person would show up for Bible study. This did not deter Mr. Eason from teaching the one-hour session. Years passed, and the Eason children married and started their families, with the exception of their youngest daughter. She worked as the church secretary with Mr. Eason. After forty years, preaching began to take a toll on Mr. Eason. He frequently fainted while preaching, and the paramedics would be notified. On the paramedic's arrival at the church, Mr. Eason would eventually become aroused, and when the paramedics proceeded to transport him to the hospital, Mr. Eason would insist he was all right and refuse to go. This went on for many months. But as months went by, Mr. Eason became so ill he had to be hospitalized. Eventually, he had to undergo hemodialysis. After Mr. Eason had been hospitalized for several weeks, he refused further treatment. He requested that he be returned to his home to spend his last days. Mr. Eason died in his home, surrounded by his family. Initially, Mrs. Eason was not informed of her husband's death , but later the family broke the news to her. The community church was so small that two funerals were held for Mr. Eason. One evening a funeral service was held at the local community church. The subsequent day, a second funeral was held at a much larger church, and over two thousand individuals attended to show their respect for Mr. Eason. Mr. Eason had obviously touched so many lives. Another giant in the community had died. I wondered how we could pay homage to this great man. I again went before three governing bodies in the county, and as a result, the street was renamed in honor of Mr. Eason.

Approximately two years after the death of Mr. Eason, Mrs. Eason died. Perhaps the thought of losing her husband of over forty years was too much for her to handle. Today, the Eason's house, once occupied by the Eason family, remains vacant. The cement blockhouse has had no major renovations; it is just as Mr. and Mrs. Edison left it. After all, their spirits rest on this sacred ground.

Chapter 19

Mr. & Mrs. Goodwin: Mother and Sons

Mr. and Mrs. Goodwin lived on the other side of the same street as the Easons. Mrs. Goodwin had a son prior to marrying Mr. Goodwin. During the early fifties, Mr. and Mrs. Goodwin lost one of seven children to leukemia. This child was no more than two years old. Mr. Goodwin was a very tall man. He was approximately 6'6" tall. Mrs. Goodwin was also very tall, about 6'6' and very thin. Mr. Goodwin performed janitorial work at the local bread company until his retirement. Mrs. Goodwin was a domestic worker. Years passed, and the Goodwin's children entered high school. One winter evening, the eldest son decided to go to the store in the city. To go to the store, one had to travel on a busy, four-lane boulevard. It was near dusk when the son, wearing a dark jacket, started out. Apparently, the first motorist didn't see him and he struck the young man. Multiple other motorists then hit the body. This was devastating to the Goodwins. But Mr. and Mrs. Goodwin were strengthened by their faith. They continued to attend weekly church services. Twenty years later, Mr. and Mrs. Goodwin's children moved away, with the exception of the youngest daughter and youngest son. Months passed, and the neighbors had not seen the youngest daughter. The community later learned the daughter had not been seen because she was pregnant. The neighbors were taken by surprise, especially since they never saw her daughter going out on dates. The daughter gave birth to a boy. Mr. and Mrs. Goodwin helped raise their grandson. As the grandson grew up and entered high school, he began to get into trouble; he was even suspended from school. Eventually, he dropped out of high school. The grandson's defiant behavior continued, which led to imprisonment. Shortly after the grandson's defiant behavior manifested, Mr. and Mrs. Goodwin's daughter began to display a behavior disorder. She stopped talking to everyone. This might have been an internal conflict, as she may have found things going on around her too much to handle. This was another challenge Mr. and Mrs. Goodwin would have to face. But it would not be the only one. Mr. and Mrs. Goodwin's faith would be tested again.

Nine years later, Mr. Goodwin began to experience back pain. When his pain became intense, he was taken to the doctor. After series of tests were done, he was diagnosed with prostate cancer. Approximately three years after he was diagnosed with prostate cancer, Mr. Goodwin died. Mrs. Goodwin grieved his death for months. Her granddaughter insisted she move out of her house and in with her. Mrs. Goodwin lived with her granddaughter for approximately ten years. Afterward, she was determined to return to her home, so Mrs. Goodwin and her daughter moved back into the family's house. Mrs. Goodwin's firstborn son moved in with her. She began to feel apart of the community again. She made major improvements to her home. She installed storm windows, and new siding was placed on the house. Her son, a former brick mason, built her a large, brick mailbox. She planted flowers in the yard, and a wooden privacy fence was installed in her backyard. But Mrs. Goodwin's faith would be tested again. Her son was arrested and was confined for two years. On release from jail, he and girlfriend moved back in with Mrs. Goodwin. She was elated to have her son back; he had been so helpful to her in the past. Also, Mrs. Goodwin welcomed her son's girlfriend to her home and made her feel a part of the family. The son's girlfriend was about thirty years his junior. Now Mrs. Goodwin, her daughter , her son, and the son's girlfriend lived together. Yet, this would be short-lived. The girlfriend frequently became ill. She had a respiratory condition that caused her breathing difficulties. An x-ray revealed she had pneumonia. Once she went to the doctor's office for a scheduled appointment. Mrs. Goodwin's son thought it was a routine doctor's appointment, but this time it would be different. She was admitted to the hospital and never returned. She died from respiratory complications. This was a shock to Mrs. Goodwin and her son. Mrs. Goodwin would grieve yet another loss. After the death of Mrs. Godwin's son's girlfriend, he was never the same. He began to drink excessively; Approximately three months after the death of his girlfriend l, he was diagnosed with prostate cancer. He lived approximately twelve months after the death of his girlfriend. Mrs. Goodwin took the loss of this son deeply -just as she did that of her son some forty years earlier. She tried to arrange the funeral, but she couldn't without the assistance of her granddaughters. The funeral was held at Mrs. Goodwin's church, since the son was not a member of a church. Mrs. Goodwin grieved for quite some time, yet she was able to muster the strength to attend church occasionally. Mrs. Goodwin, who is in her nineties, suffered a stroke a year ago. She is now confined to a wheelchair. Her daughter and her youngest son live in the old homestead. After all, this is sacred ground.

Epilogue

Reflection

These are the neighbors who had the most profound affect on my life. There were other individuals who are not mentioned in this book. They, too, were as integral to this sacred community as those who were included. As I conclude this story, I do so with a bit of sadness. This book may be the only tangible thing left to remember our ancestors, friends, and neighbors once resided on this sacred ground. As I look around, I see the construction of new townhomes and large, single-family homes, and new faces. But the new residents will not understand the significance and the many sacrifices made by those who have gone before them. They will not comprehend how many nights our ancestors were awakened by the Klansmen's activities, such as throwing burning crosses in their yards and shouting racial remarks as they drove by on a dirt road that is now paved and illuminated by streetlights. They will not view this community as sacred. They will never understand how one spring day in 1955, after my brother and I missed the school bus, my brother, out of complete boredom, decided to make a slingshot. He wanted to show me how skillful he was in mastering it. Unfortunately, my brother's targets would be birds in the woods. I followed him into the woods next to the cemetery. He ordered me to remain silent as he released his ammunition and barely missing a bird. A shepherd suddenly appeared! I asked my brother where he come from. I realize today that what my brother and I saw was not from this present world. He was about six feet tall, with snow-white hair and beard, which extended below his waist. His robe was so white it was almost blinding. He had a rope tied around his waist, and in his right hand, he held a staff, which extended about two inches above his head. We ran out of those woods and did not stop until we were home. We both remember that event as if it happened yesterday. And who could ever forget the many conversations we had with the gravedigger who lived and worked in the cemetery. He often described how a young girl appeared every day about 3:00 p.m., kneel, and then vanish right before his eyes. I imagine this gravedigger, who had lived in the cemetery all of his life, had seen more things than anyone could ever imagine. He would tell us how he dug graves for the unknowns who were brought to the cemetery by men in uniforms. Looking back, I wonder if these unknown corpses were those had been lynched. There were many lynching that occurred during that era. I began to think that could be the reason my father, uncles, and aunts refused to talk when we questioned them about the cause of death of an uncle who died years earlier. This uncle could have been among the unknowns buried in this same cemetery. (I recently learned from an older relative this particular uncle was taken away from my father's family at approximately eighteen years of age by a group of white males, and he was never to be seen again. My grandparents were told if they went to the local authorities, the entire family would be killed.) In this community today, there are paupers' graves, many who are unknown. And who could ever forget the ghoul dressed in an oversized coat and a top hat that paced back and forth in our backyard late one night. This ghoul would not be intimidated no matter how many times my father fired his automatic shotgun into the air. The ghoul danced back and forth, from side to side, until he vanished into the cemetery located at the end of our backyard. And we will never forget how, as children while walking in the community late one night, a white, round object crossed our path and vanished before our eyes. We shall remember this rich land, especially the families who demonstrated great wisdom, fortitude, determination, and exuberant strength in their faith in God. The community will remain a very special place for those of us who grew up there, and regardless of how the community transitions, it will always remain sacred ground.

Printed in the United States
126363LV00005B/1/P